How to Trade
Put and Call Options
The New and Proven Way to
Stock Market Profits

How to Trade
Put and Call Options
The New and Proven Way to
Stock Market Profits

Lawrence R. Rosen

 1974

Dow Jones-Irwin, Inc.   Homewood, Illinois   60430

First Printing, September 1974

ISBN 0-87094-076-7
Library of Congress Catalog Card No. 74-81385

Printed in the United States of America

Preface

Are you weary of buying stocks and waiting for them to go up before making a profit?

Are you tired of "selling short" and not making money unless and until the stock declines?

If so, then options may present a desirable alternative method of investing.

Under normal circumstances, when one buys a stock, in two out of three possible occurrences the investor makes no profit, i.e., if the stock goes down or remains the same; he only profits if the stock increases in price. And he has no protection against loss in an adverse price movement.

Selling options on stocks owned or purchased allows the investor the possibility of handsome annual rates of return (frequently 40 percent per annum or more) in two out of three possible events—if the stock remains at the purchase price or if it increases. And, a buffer of protection against loss exists in the event that the stock declines.

For more venturesome investors, annualized rates of

return of 100 percent and more are possible under "bear-ish" market situations by selling "naked" options (without buying any stock). In this instance the investor again realizes such profits in two out of three eventualities—if the stock involved either remains the same or declines. And, a buffer of protection against loss exists in the event of an adverse stock price increase.

When one borrows money from a bank, the bank usually collects its interest in advance. Thus the bank not only receives interest for the period of the loan, it has in addition the interest to invest during the period of the loan.

In a similar manner, the option writer—who sells options on securities—collects premiums in advance and the writer has the premium monies so collected available to invest during the option period.

The author has negotiated hundreds of thousands of dollars of option transactions, both as a registered repre-sentative of one of the largest New York Stock Exchange member firms and subsequently as a private business for his own account.

Options represent an intriguing investment media and one which has been unnecessarily clouded in mystery. The purpose of this book is to expose the risks and rewards that options can provide so that all potential investors may better understand the possibilities that exist in this excit-ing field.

Special thanks are due for their helpful review to Everett Moffat, president, and William Lewke, vice president, Ragnar Option Corp., Barbara Kaplan of the Chicago Board Options Exchange, and to Ronald Abrams, tax partner at Coopers & Lybrand, Certified Public Accoun-tants, for his comments regarding taxation. The author of course assumes responsibility for the text, and any errors or omissions.

August 1974   LAWRENCE R. ROSEN

Contents

1

Instant Profits–
Buying a Stock and
Writing a Call

A substantial demand exists on the part of the investing public for *call options* on securities.

A call option is simply a contract that gives the buyer the right (i.e., the option) to acquire 100 shares of a particular stock at a specified price, called the *striking price,* or exercise price. The option is valid for a specified duration; usually six months and ten days. Other common durations are 35 days, 65 days, 95 days and one year. The striking price is normally the current market price (last trade on the exchange) at the moment when the option contract is negotiated.

For every option that is bought by the public, another individual or institution acts as the seller. Let's explore the call option seller's position. He is selling an option to someone else and the seller therefore must be prepared to deliver 100 shares of the stock, upon the demand of the option buyer during the agreed time period and against delivery of cash in the specified amount. Let us regard an actual case of a negotiated option transaction that took place on August 9, 1972.

The option seller bought 500 shares of Kingsford (Stock Exchange symbol KFD) at 13⅞ ($13.875)[1] per share and simultaneously sold five call options, exercisable at 13⅞ for a 65-day period. The option seller received a *premium* of $750.00 ($150 per hundred shares) from the buyer. The economic effect to the seller is as follows.

Cost price of 500 shares at 13⅞ $6,937.50
Plus: brokerage cost to buy 500 shares 114.44
Gross cash outlay 7,051.94
Less: premium received from sale of options, net 750.00
Option seller's actual cash outlay without use of
  margin (credit) $6,301.94

It is against the cash outlay, in this case $6,301.94, that we seek to measure the option seller's potential profit from this transaction.

At the time the option seller acquired the 500 Kingsford shares he was assured of receiving a $750 net premium resulting from his sale of five call options covering the 500 shares. This net premium income represents instant gross revenue to him. However, if the option is exercised by the buyer, the price paid per share (13⅞) to the seller will not include the brokerage commission originally charged to the option seller, nor will the 13⅞ include compensation to the seller for the costs charged by his New York Stock Exchange firm for handling the sale. These additional costs include: (a) brokerage; (b) New York transfer tax, either at the resident rate or at a lesser rate for nonresidents of New York state, and (c) the SEC fee.[2] Thus, the net

---

[1] Prices of securities are ordinarily given in *points;* each point is equivalent to $1 with respect to stocks; $10 with respect to bonds.
[2] Brokerage costs, etc., change periodically, and those expressed throughout the text should not be regarded as current by the reader.

premium income must be reduced by the above three expenses—which will be incurred if the option is exercised. The actual computation follows:

Net premium income		$750.00
Less:		
Brokerage cost to buy	$114.44	
Brokerage cost to sell	114.44	
N.Y. transfer tax (nonresident)	12.18	
SEC fee	0.14	
Total deductions		241.20
Net profit		$508.80

Shown below is the traditional debit and credit account which should make it easier to grasp the derivation of the $508.80 potential profit from this transaction.

	Debits	Credits
Purchase 500 KFD	$6,937.50	
Brokerage on purchase	114.44	
Sold 5 call options		$ 750.00
Options exercised:		
Sell 500 KFD		6,937.50
Brokerage on sale	114.44	
N.Y. transfer tax (nonresident) on sale	12.18	
SEC fee on sale	0.14	
Totals	$7,178.70	$7,687.50
Balance		$ 508.80

The key concept in investing is percentage return on invested capital; $508.80 would be a miserable profit on tying up, let us say, $100,000 for a year. But is it a good rate of return in the Kingsford transaction? Let's see.

The option seller's cash outlay was $6,301.94. His net profit, if the option is exercised, is $508.80. The duration of the option is 65 days. Assume that the option is exercised on the last possible day—the 65th day (which produces the least possible rate of return to the option seller, providing the option is exercised). The seller's rate of annualized return is computed as follows:

$$\text{Annualized profit} = \left[\frac{\text{Profit (508.80)}}{\text{Cash outlay (6,301.94)}}\right]\left[\frac{365 \text{ (days per year)}}{65 \text{ (option days)}}\right]$$

$$= \frac{508.80}{6,301.94} \times \frac{365}{65}$$

$$= \underline{45.3\%}$$

Thus 45.3 percent is the annualized rate of return, or the annual percentage return to the option seller before personal income taxes.

There is no question that the option seller had the $750 in hand at the start of the transaction—hence the title of this chapter—"instant profits." However, as we shall now see, this instant profit or more will be actually realized: (a) if the stock rises above 13⅞ and the options are exercised, and (b) if the option is not exercised—and if, at the option expiry date, (i) the option seller disposes of the stock at the option price or higher or (ii) sells a new option at the option price or higher. The rate of return *could* actually be much *higher* than 45.3 percent to the option seller. This would occur if the option is exercised before its expiry date. For example, if the Kingsford option were exercised after only 32 days the rate of return would be doubled, to about 90.6 percent per annum.

At the time when the option expires, if the stock is below the original cost, the rate of return will be reduced. A loss would be incurred if the value of the stock is below the original cost less the premium income plus brokerage costs to buy and sell, New York transfer tax, and SEC fee.

The break-even point in terms of price per share at the option expiry date would be determined in the following manner.

```
Original cost per share..........................  13⅞
Premium income ....................  $750.00
Less:
  Brokerage cost to buy and sell .........    228.88
  N.Y. transfer tax and SEC fee .........     12.32
Net profit if option exercised ...........    508.80
```

$$\text{Net profit per share if option exercised} = \frac{508.80}{500 \text{ shares}} = \$1.01.$$

The downside buffer of protection enjoyed by the option seller is $1.01. He could sell out at the option expiry date at a price of 13⅞ less $1.01 and still break even, before considering any personal income tax consequences. If he sold out at a price above 12⅞ but less than 13⅞, his annualized rate of return would be between 0 and 45.3 percent. Only if he were to sell out at the option expiry date at a price below 12⅞ would the option seller suffer a loss.

Now let us examine the economic consequences to the option seller in the transaction.

Event	Effect on Option Seller
KFD goes up and option is exercised at expiry	Annualized profit is 45.3%
KFD goes up and option is exercised before expiry	Annualized profit is greater than 45.3%
KFD is unchanged (at 13⅞) at option expiry and is sold at that price or a new option is written at that striking price or higher..................	Annualized profit is 45.3% or better*

---

*At this point we see that the option seller has made a handsome profit even though his stock remains at the purchase price. This is a key advantage to option writing. (This advantage is offset by the fact that the option seller's profit—in this case 45.3 percent—is limited irrespective of how large the increase may be in the price of his stock during the option period.)

Event (Continued)	Effect on Option Seller
KFD declines to 12⅞ at option expiry and stock is sold	Zero profit
KFD declines below 12⅞ at option expiry and stock is sold	A loss is incurred

The option writer is usually more conservative in nature than the option buyer. The seller's main interests are generally preservation of capital and an adequate return, while, on the other hand, the buyer may be seeking great speculative profits. The seller gives up the chance to make very large speculative profits—i.e., any profit in excess of the option premium—and by so doing obtains downside protection.

Use of Margin Credit to Sell a Call on a "Rapid Mover." A seller of calls never knows in advance when he has picked a "rapid mover"—i.e., a stock that gains sharply, inducing the option buyer to exercise his option much earlier than the option expiry date. Such a rapid mover for one of my clients was Rapid-American (RPD), the retail conglomerate. My client had the good fortune to benefit from the following transaction.

Date	Transaction	Amount Paid or Received
10/2/72	Bought 300 RPD @ 15, cost	$4,580.50
10/2/72	Sold 3 calls expiring 4/12/73; striking price 15, premium net received	562.50

On December 29, 1972, the three calls were exercised; sales proceeds were $4,412.50. My client made the purchase on October 2, 1972, using full margin, with a 55-percent margin requirement. The economic effect was:

Cash Outlay

Cost of 300 shares	$4,580.50
55% of $4,580.50 margin requirement (cash required to be deposited with broker)	2,519.27*
Less: premium income	(562.50)
Cash outlay	$1,956.78

Loan (from Broker)

Cost	$4,580.50
Margin requirement	(2,519.27)
Loan	$2,061.23

Profit

Sales proceeds ($4,580.50 less costs of sale)	$4,419.50
Plus: premium income	562.50
Less: interest on $2,061.23 for 89 days @ 6.5%*...	(32.67)
Subtotal	$4,949.33
Less: cost	(4,580.50)
Profit	$ 368.83

Annualized Return on Investment

$$\frac{368.83 \text{ (profit)}}{1,956.78 \text{ (cash outlay)}} \times \frac{365 \text{ (days)}}{89 \text{ (days)}} = \underline{\underline{77.3\%}}$$

*Margin requirements change periodically, as do interest rates.

The magnitude of the return was so great because the option buyer had paid a premium for six months ten days but exercised the option in just under 90 days. The option seller then received a six-month-ten-day premium for the less than 90-day period that his money was actually tied up.

The transactions that we have just examined are actual (not hypothetical) option transactions, and profits of the magnitude shown are frequently available to option writers at the inception of a transaction. It should be apparent that the option writer's risk is only on the downside with respect to the stock he purchases in order to execute an option sale. A severe decline in the acquired stock could cause a huge loss to the option writer, and the buffer of protection he enjoys from receiving premium income would be of small solace. Thus, it is obvious that "option writing" is not a panacea and it is of paramount importance to success that for this type of transaction the option writer endeavor to select stocks, for the purpose of option writing, that he feels have minimum or reduced downside risk.

The traditional methods of stock selection, including both fundamental and technical analysis, are as important to the success of an option-writing program as they are to conventional investing.

2

Treatment of Dividends and Distributions

In chapter 1, the basic principles of writing call options were discussed. However, it is necessary to consider the effect on the option writer of various distributions such as cash dividends, rights issues, and stock dividends, that go "ex" during the option period. Normally, the ex-date for a distribution is the fourth business day preceding the "record date." All stockholders of record on the "record date" are entitled to the particular distribution.

On the day that a stock sells ex-dividend on the exchange, the striking price of all outstanding call options (not traded on an exchange) is reduced in price by the amount by which the stock sells ex-dividend. For example, a call with a striking price of 50 is automatically reduced to a striking price of 49 on the day that the stock sells ex-dividend of $1.00. The $1.00 dividend is paid to the option seller who is long (owns) the stock—as he is the stockholder on the record date. However, although the option seller actually receives the dividend, in the event that the call option sold is in fact exercised, he loses the benefit of the dividend as the result of the reduction in the striking price from 50 to 49.

On the other hand, if the call option is *not* exercised, the option seller retains full benefit of the dividends he receives including those that went "ex-dividend" during the option period. Such dividends, of course, add to the writer's downside protection. Simply stated, all distributions that go "ex" during the option period accrue to the option buyer at the expense of the seller, if and only if he exercises the option.

When stock dividends go "ex" during the option period, the terms of the option provide for the number of shares covered thereunder to be increased by the dividend shares. For example, an option is sold for 100 shares of Vornado, Inc. The company goes "ex" a 7-percent-stock dividend during the option period. The option now is for 107 shares rather than the original 100.

3

The Call Option Contract

The terms of the standard call option contract are illustrated by the following example.

New York, N.Y.   (April 1)   19 (74)

For value received, the BEARER may CALL on the ENDORSER for one hundred (100) shares of the (COMMON) stock of the (Pet, Inc.) at (forty) dollars ($40.00) per share any time within (six months and ten days) from date. This stock option contract must be presented, as specified below, to the endorsing firm before the expiration of the exact time limit. It cannot be exercised by telephone.

During the life of this option: 1. (a) The contract price shall be reduced by the value of any cash dividend on the day the stock goes ex-dividend; (b) where the option is entitled to rights and/or warrants the contract price shall be reduced by the value of same as fixed by the opening sale thereof on the day the stock sells ex-rights and/or warrants. 2. (a) in the event of stock splits, reverse splits, or other similar action by the above-mentioned corporation, this option shall become an option for the equivalent in new securities when duly listed for trading and the total contract price shall not be reduced; (b) stock dividends or the equivalent due-bills shall be attached to the stock covered hereby when and if this option is exercised and the total contract price shall not be reduced.

Upon presentation to the ENDORSER of this option attached to a comparison ticket in the manner and time specified, the ENDORSER agrees to accept notice of the BEARER's exercise by stamping the comparison, and this acknowledgment shall constitute a contract and shall be controlling with respect to delivery of the stock and settlement in accordance with New York Stock Exchange usage.

Expires (October 11) 19 (74)

Sold by member
Put & Call
Brokers & Dealers
Association, Inc.

The undersigned acts as intermediary only, without obligation other than to obtain a New York Stock Exchange firm as endorser.

[signature of put and call dealer]

Note that the option contract is between "the bearer" and a New York Stock Exchange firm which by endorsing the option guarantees that the option seller will fulfill his commitment if "called" upon to do so. After endorsement, the contract is retained by the brokerage firm representing the option buyer. Neither the name of the option seller nor that of the option buyer physically appears on the option contract. In some instances the buyer of the option may be directly from one of the many members of the Put and Call Broker Dealers Association, Inc. Even in that case, the contract is still submitted to the New York Stock Exchange firm of the option seller's choice for endorsement. Shown in figures 3-1 and 3-2 are the face and reverse sides of an actual call option contract.

12

FIGURE 3-1

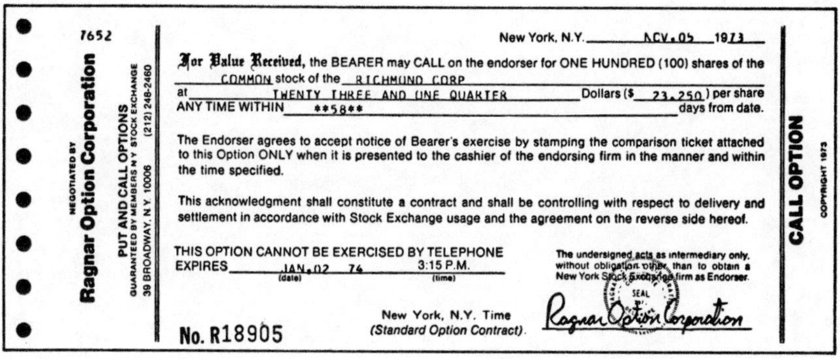

7652

NEGOTIATED BY
Ragnar Option Corporation
PUT AND CALL OPTIONS
GUARANTEED BY MEMBERS N Y STOCK EXCHANGE
39 BROADWAY, N.Y. 10006 (212) 248-2460

New York, N.Y. NOV. 05 1973

For Value Received, the BEARER may CALL on the endorser for ONE HUNDRED (100) shares of the COMMON stock of the RICHMOND CORP at TWENTY THREE AND ONE QUARTER Dollars ($ 23.250) per share ANY TIME WITHIN **58** days from date.

The Endorser agrees to accept notice of Bearer's exercise by stamping the comparison ticket attached to this Option ONLY when it is presented to the cashier of the endorsing firm in the manner and within the time specified.

This acknowledgment shall constitute a contract and shall be controlling with respect to delivery and settlement in accordance with Stock Exchange usage and the agreement on the reverse side hereof.

THIS OPTION CANNOT BE EXERCISED BY TELEPHONE
EXPIRES JAN. 02 74 (date) 3:15 P.M. (time)

The undersigned acts as intermediary only, without obligation other than to obtain a New York Stock Exchange firm as Endorser.

SEAL

New York, N.Y. Time
(Standard Option Contract)

Ragnar Option Corporation

No. R18905

CALL OPTION

COPYRIGHT 1973

FIGURE 3-2

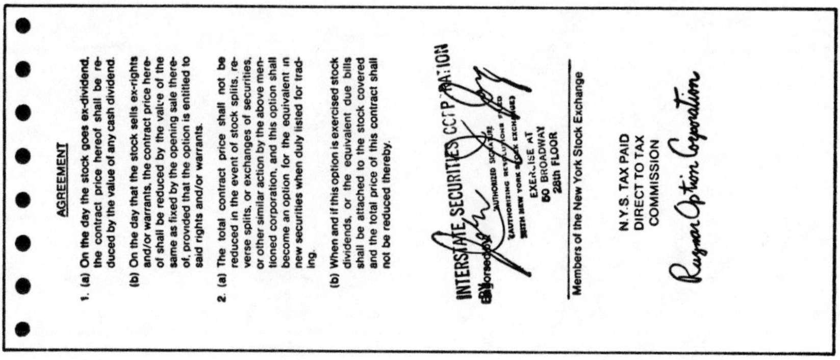

AGREEMENT

1. (a) On the day the stock goes ex-dividend, the contract price hereof shall be reduced by the value of any cash dividend.

(b) On the day that the stock sells ex-rights and/or warrants, the contract price hereof shall be reduced by the value of the same as fixed by the opening sale thereof, provided that the option is entitled to said rights and/or warrants.

2. (a) The total contract price shall not be reduced in the event of stock splits, reverse splits, or exchanges of securities, or other similar action by the above mentioned corporation, and this option shall become an option for the equivalent in new securities when duly listed for trading.

(b) When and if this option is exercised stock dividends, or the equivalent due bills shall be attached to the stock covered and the total price of this contract shall not be reduced thereby.

INTERSTATE SECURITIES CORPORATION
Endorsed By
AUTHORIZED SIGNATURE
AUTHORIZING REGULATIONS FILED WITH NEW YORK STOCK EXCHANGE
EXERCISE AT
50 BROADWAY
28th FLOOR

Members of the New York Stock Exchange

N.Y.S. TAX PAID
DIRECT TO TAX
COMMISSION

Ragnar Option Corporation

4

Option Writing
for the
Locked-In Investor

The nature of U.S. federal income tax laws tends to act as a disturbing force in portfolio management. There are innumerable instances of investors—in their youth and peak earnings periods—acquiring judiciously excellent growth stocks such as IBM, Avon, Kresge, Warner-Lambert, and Xerox. At the time of purchase the investor is essentially interested in long-term growth rather than current dividend income.

As the years pass, the stocks appreciate substantially in value, and at some point the investor finds himself in his 60s or 70s with substantial assets—in terms of market value—but with little in the way of percentage yield from actual dividends relative to the market value of his portfolio.

Human nature is such that the investor, who now desires current income from dividends and interest, is loath to sell securities from his portfolio because of the capital gains tax laws—even though such gains would ordinarily be taxed at favorable rates.

A person in this position, who will not sell portfolio assets, has an ideal opportunity to achieve his objectives by selling call options against his existing portfolio holdings. For example, an investor owns 100 shares of XYZ with a present market value of $40,000. The annual dividends amount to $540, which is 1.35 percent of the market value.

Assume that the investor could sell a one-year call option for a net premium of $5,000. Only two events may occur—the option lapses or it is exercised. If the option lapses, the investor is simply $5,000 better off than he would have been otherwise. If the option is exercised, the investor will not—repeat not—sell the 100 shares of XYZ which he owned at the time he sold the option. Instead he purchases 100 new shares of XYZ on the market on the day the option is exercised and delivers those newly purchased shares against receipt of the agreed striking price proceeds. For example, one year later, XYZ rises to $420 and the buyer exercises his right to acquire 100 shares at $400 each.

Investor buys 100 at $420 = $42,000

Investor sells 100 at $400 = $40,000

The tax effect of the transaction is that the net premium income from the sale of the option of $5,000 is added to the sales proceeds of $40,000, total $45,000.[1] Deducting the cost price of $42,000, the investor realizes a short-term capital gain of $3,000. This corresponds to a cash flow to the investor of $5,000 premium income less $2,000 loss on the purchase and sale.

Assume the XYZ rose in value to $500 per share at the

---

[1] $45,000 would be reduced by the dividends which went "ex" during the option period.

Brokerage costs are neglected as are the New York transfer tax and SEC fee.

expiration of the year option period. Then, the investor would buy 100 shares for $50,000 and sell the same for $40,000. After adding the $5,000 premium to the sales proceeds, the investor experiences a cash flow deficit and short-term capital loss of $5,000. This cash flow deficit may be met by selling enough of his low-yielding portfolio to produce a $5,000 capital gain. If the cost basis for the stock he sells is 50 percent of the present market value, he could sell $10,000 from the portfolio, use $5,000 to bring his cash and tax position to zero, and have freed $5,000 to invest in higher-yielding stocks or bonds.

Thus it appears that a "locked-in" investor, who would not sell from his portfolio because of tax implications, benefits handsomely by selling options irrespective of market price developments. If the option lapses, he is ahead by the premium income (i.e., $5,000). If the option is exercised, and the premium income (i.e., $5,000) exceeds the rise in the price of the stock (e.g., $2,000) he is ahead by the difference (e.g., $3,000). Only in the event that the rise in stock price (e.g., $10,000) exceeds the premium income (i.e., $5,000) would his total assets have been greater by not selling the option. But, even in the later case, he has the peripheral benefit of converting tax-free some (i.e., $5,000) low-yield assets to those which have a higher yield.

5

Why Buyers Buy Calls

Perhaps the most frequent reason why people buy call options on a stock is that they have some particular reason to be extremely optimistic about the prospects for increase in the value of a security in the short term. Reports have appeared in the *Wall Street Journal* from time to time of enormous profits that have been realized by the purchasers of call options on such stocks as Winnebago and Vetco Offshore Industries, Inc.

The author has noticed that in several instances option buyers appeared shortly before merger announcements as in the case of Kingsford and National General Corporation. (Nevertheless, insiders are subject to various constraints pursuant to federal securities law in acting upon inside information.)

Call options may also be purchased for other reasons such as a means of investing with risk limited to a specific sum paid to acquire the option. A call option might also be purchased by someone who views the outlook for a stock quite negatively. In this instance the individual would sell the stock short and simultaneously purchase a call option. If the stock rises, the loss on the short sale is balanced by the profit on the call option. The investor would lose brokerage commissions and the premium paid for the call option. But if the stock drops sharply, the investor would profit by the decline to the extent that it exceeds the premium paid for the call option and brokerage costs. (A "bearish" investor might fare better by buying a "put"—an option to sell.) The intriguing possibilities that exist in buying call options compared to buying the stock are illustrated in the accompanying matrix, which compares the results of three specified situations in the event that the price of a security increases, remains the same, or decreases.

As shown in the table there are advantages and disadvantages in buying options versus owning the stock, which include the following.

Some Advantages in Buying Options. (1) With an option purchase $400 can control 100 shares of stock while a $4,000 investment would be required to purchase 100 shares of the same stock outright. (2) The option buyer can control 100 shares with risk limited to $400, while the stock purchaser's risk is theoretically $4,000. (3) The option buyer has the potential of greater profits if his investment judgment is correct—as shown in event A. The option buyer in this case could make 150 percent return on his investment in circumstances in which the stock buyer would make only 25 percent.

Some Advantages of Owning the Stock. (1) The stock owner loses nothing if the stock remains unchanged; the option buyer loses everything in this case. (2) If the price of the stock remains unchanged (or drops) the stock owner receives dividends; the owner of an unexercised option receives no benefit from dividends.

Buying Calls for Trading Purposes. One of my clients purchased four calls on Chrysler stock on November 3,

Option Buying Versus Stock Buying*

Situation / Event	1	2	3	Remarks
	Buy 100 shares at $40. Total investment—$4,000	Buy call options (10) on 1,000 shares, at cost of $400 per option. Total investment—$4,000	Buy one option on 100 shares, exercisable at $40, premium $400. Total investment—$400	
A During option period stock increases to $50 and the stock is sold or the option is exercised.	Profit = $10 per share × 100 shares, i.e., $1,000. Percent return 25	Profit is 1,000 × $10 per share, $10,000 less the cost of the 10 options, $4,000, i.e., $6,000. Percent return 150	Profit is 100 shares × $10 per share less the $400 cost of the option, i.e., $600. Percent return 150	The option buyers fare much better than the buyer of the stock.
B During option period stock remains unchanged at $40 and the stock is sold and option expires.	Profit .... $0 Percent return 0	Loss .... $4,000 Percent loss 100	Loss .... $400 Percent loss....... 100	The buyer of the stock fared better than the option buyers, who both lost their investment.
C During option period stock decreases to $20 and stock is sold and option expires unexercised.	Loss .... $2,000 Percent loss..... 50	Loss .... $4,000 Percent loss..... 100	Loss .... $400 Percent loss 100	The option buyer in Situation 3 loses 100%, but limited his risk to $400.

*For simplicity, brokerage costs and personal income tax consequences are ignored.

1972. The options were exercisable at 35½ and expired six months and ten days later. Each option cost $350, so that the cost of the four totaled $1,400, to which was added a New York transfer tax of $5 per call; this made the overall investment $1,420. On December 7, 1972, when the price of Chrysler stock had climbed to 41½, my client decided to sell short 400 shares at 41½, providing sales proceeds of $16,391.26.[1] His reasoning was that the price of the stock had reached its peak in the short term and that he would be able to cover his short sale at a lower price in the near future and still have several months for the price to recover, again, before his four calls expired. At this point, he was in a riskless position because if the price of the stock increased from 41½, his additional gain from the four calls was balanced by his loss on the short sale, and, if the price of the stock decreased, his profit from the short sale was balanced by the reduced value of his calls.[2] In the event that the investor remained in this posture until the calls were due to expire, the effect would have been to freeze his gain from the purchase of the calls at 41½ less 35½, or six points per share before the cost of the options and expenses. This is true because before the calls expired he would sell the calls for his profit (or exercise them) and cover his short sale.

Buying a Call on a High-Yield Stock. The buyer of a call option benefits by all dividends through an automatic reduction in the striking price in the amount of the dividends on their "ex" date. One can purchase, as did several of my clients, a six-month-ten-day call just before the ex-dividend date. In this way, the option buyer receives the benefit of three dividends during the option period of six months and ten days. One particular case involved

---

[1] Margin requirements must be met on the short sale.
[2] At prices below the call "striking" price he derives additional profit from the short sale.

Gulf Oil, which has a long and steady history of paying $37.50 per quarter per 100 shares in dividends. The ex-dates historically have been almost exactly three months apart. On January 22, 1973, my client bought one call on Gulf Oil for six months and ten days, expiring on August 1, 1973, and exercisable at 28⅞ for a net premium, including transfer tax, of $255.

It is expected that three dividends of $37.50 will go "ex" during the option period, a total of $112.50, or 1⅛ per share. Thus the striking price is expected to be adjusted to 28⅞ less 1⅛, or 27¾. In effect then, counting the expected dividend benefit, if the option is exercised the cost has been $255 less $112.50, or only $142.50.

If the option does not show a profit as completion of the six-month period nears, the option buyer can sell the option for $1 and realize a short-term capital loss of the entire $255. For an investor in the 50-percent tax bracket, who can utilize up to $1,000 of short-term capital losses as a deduction from ordinary income, his after-tax risk then is only 50 percent of $255, or $127.50.

On the other hand, if the price of the stock moves up, let us say 10 points, the situation is as follows:

Original striking price 28⅞
Reduction for dividends 1⅛
New striking price 27¾
Market price at option expiry date 38⅞

The option buyer then sells the option back to his broker for the profit less a round-trip commission; i.e., the brokerage cost including transfer tax and SEC fee to both buy at 27¾ and sell at 38⅞. The following analysis describes the transaction.

Gross profit: 100 shares times $(38\% - 27\frac{3}{4})$ $1,112.50
Less:
  Brokerage cost to buy 100 @ $27\frac{3}{4}$ .... (46.98)
  Brokerage cost, transfer tax and SEC fee for
    sale at 38% .... (60.32)
  Original cost of option .... (255.00)
Profit .... $ 750.20

Percentage Return. The profit of $750.20 represents a 536.7 percent annualized return on the original investment of $255. Moreover, the profit is a long-term capital gain— since the option was held more than six months before it was sold back to the broker. At 25-percent long-term capital gains tax rates, the reward potential after tax is $562.65, compared to a loss risk after tax of $127.50.

An interesting facet of this maneuver is that the three dividends declared "ex" during the option period were converted to long-term capital gains as far as the option buyer was concerned.

6

Federal Income Tax Consequences to the Seller and Buyer of a Call Option

The Buyer

An investor pays a premium to acquire a call option for a specified duration. There are three potential events that may occur: (1) The option simply expires or lapses; (2) the option itself is sold later by its original owner; and (3) the option is exercised. Each case has its own distinct tax treatment.

The Option Simply Lapses. Lapse of the option could occur if the option buyer finds that the price of the stock on which he purchased the option is below the option striking price, is the same as the striking price, or is not sufficiently above the striking price to cover brokerage costs. At the moment when the option lapses or expires a taxable event takes place. The premium previously paid becomes a capital loss. Generally, the loss is long-term or short-term depending upon the length of time it was held by the investor. A call option held for more than six months that expires is a long-term capital loss. If an option expires and the holding period was six months or less, the loss is short-term.

The Option Itself Is Sold Later. There are at least two reasons why an option buyer may find it preferable to sell the option itself. Let us say that a call option is acquired on a stock at $100 per share for six months and ten days. Shortly before six months and one day have elapsed from the date of purchase of the option, the stock is trading at 60. Chances of a recovery to 100 within 10 or 11 days appear to be remote. If the option owner maintains his ownership of the option more than six months, his capital loss is long-term, but if he sells the option to a third party—e.g., his brokerage firm—for $1.00, and the sale is made six months or less measured from the date of purchase, his capital loss is short-term. A short-term loss is more valuable (to the loser) than a long-term loss because net long-term losses may be deducted against ordinary income only on a $2 for $1 basis; i.e., it takes $2 of long-term loss to deduct $1 from ordinary income. The maximum such deduction from ordinary income is $1,000 per year.

On the other hand net short-term capital losses in excess of capital gains may be deducted up to $1,000 per year from ordinary income on a dollar for dollar basis.

Selling the Option Rather Than Exercising It. It is also desirable to sell a profitable call option as opposed to exercising it. For example, a call option for six months and ten days is purchased exercisable at $50 per share. Six months and five days later, the stock involved is at 80. If the option is exercised, the cost basis for the stock is the sum of $50 per share plus the premium per share paid to acquire the call that was exercised. However, the holding period for purposes of determining whether gains are long-term or short-term starts on the date the stock was acquired by exercise of the option. Thus, in the above case, if the option were to be exercised more than six months after its acquisition, and the stock thereby obtained were immediately sold, the capital gain would be short-term. On the other hand, the more desirable approach would be to sell the option itself; the gain, in that case, would be long-term provided the option were sold more than six months after the date it was purchased.

Most exchange member firms are willing to purchase profitable options from their clients. The price paid is the precise profit that the option holding represents (market price less striking price). However, from this amount the broker will deduct "round-trip" brokerage commissions; i.e., the same costs that the investor would have incurred if he had bought the stock by exercising the option and subsequently or simultaneously had sold the stock. Thus these costs are the brokerage costs to buy at the striking price, the brokerage costs to sell at present market price, and the New York transfer tax and the SEC fee.

The Option Is Exercised. As mentioned earlier, when an investor exercises a call, the premium paid to acquire the option is added to the price paid to buy the stock through exercise of the call option. An investor might elect this alternative if he had purchased a 95-day call that turned out to be profitable. Sale of the profitable call would be a short-term capital gain. He may instead exercise the call and acquire the stock, expecting to wait more than six months thereafter before selling.

The Seller or Writer of Calls

A call option seller receives an immediate cash payment of the premium. Nevertheless, such receipts are deferred assets and are not subject to current taxation until the related option either is exercised or expires. At that moment, when the option is exercised or expires, the deferred asset becomes taxable income in that tax year. The nature of the income, depending on the circumstances, may be either long-term capital gain, short-term capital gain, or ordinary income. It is impossible to determine at the moment of the transaction (sale of the call) which of the above types of income will result. Long-term capital gain will occur when the call option is exercised provided the stock the seller delivers has been held more than six months.

The premium received by the call option seller is added to the sales proceeds received for the stock when the option is exercised. For example, one sells a call for one year for a premium of $1,000 on 100 shares of stock, purchased simultaneously for $5,000; no dividends are paid and the striking price is $50 per share. The option is exercised nine months later. The sales proceeds are considered to be $6,000; i.e., the premium plus the amount received at the time of sale. The capital gain is long-term.

Creation of Tax Loss When Option Is Exercised. A short-term tax loss may be created in the aforementioned example. Upon exercise of the call at 50, the option seller might have chosen to retain the original shares he acquired at 50 and instead elect to satisfy the call by buying a new lot of 100 shares to deliver at the then market price; e.g., $90 per share. The results would be as follows (neglecting brokerage costs and SEC fee and New York transfer tax):

Purchase 100 shares at 90, total $9,000
Sell 100 shares at 50 plus $1,000 premium 6,000
Short-term capital loss $3,000

This loss is first utilized to offset short-term gains, then long-term gains; then up to $1,000 may be deducted from ordinary income on a dollar for dollar basis, and any remaining unused loss can be carried forward to future tax years.

Since the investor still retains the 100 shares originally purchased at $50, with a total cost of $5,000, his $3,000 deductible short-term capital loss is more than offset by untaxed unrealized capital gains (long-term in this case) of $4,000. This $4,000 is the increase in market value of the retained 100 shares from $5,000 to $9,000. The net results from the above transaction are:

Short-term deductible capital loss $3,000
Currently untaxed appreciation   4,000

Under present legislation, the $4,000 may never be subject to income tax if the investor retains those shares until death, donates them to charity, or disposes of them by gift.

Short-Term Capital Gain. As we have seen, short-term capital gains occur when a call is exercised and the stock which is delivered to satisfy the call has been held six months or less. In this case, too, the premium is added to the amount received at the time of sale to determine the sales proceeds.

Ordinary Income. Ordinary income occurs when an investor sells a call option that subsequently expires unexercised. It matters not whether the duration of the option has been more than or less than six months.

Dividend income received by the option seller is also ordinary income to him subject to the normal provisions for such dividends, including the $100 or $200 per year dividend exclusion, the 85 percent "dividend received credit" for corporations and tax-free return of capital dividends from certain real estate investment trusts or utilities.

7

Margin Accounts and Their Role in Selling Calls

The sale of a call option usually takes place in a margin account. Since a stock exchange member firm has endorsed the option contract, the buyer of the option looks to the member firm for satisfaction. In turn, the member firm looks to the option writer. In the event that an option buyer decides to exercise an option at a time when the option seller may be unavailable or unreachable the member firm must be free to deliver the optioned securities against payment. The option agreement that every margin account holder signs (as well as the margin agreement) gives very broad authority to the member firm and such authority, among many other things, would allow the member firm to deliver optioned securities from the option writer's account without his approval.

Although option sales usually take place in a margin account, there is no requirement that credit actually be utilized by the option writer. Many option writers never use credit; others do. Credit, then, may or may not be used as decided by the option writer.

Margin refers to the buying of securities on credit. The use of credit, extended by brokers, allows investors to have greater leverage in their investments—profits will be magnified as will losses in relation to the amount of cash utilized by the investor. Brokers charge interest rates of not less than 0.5 percent over the call loan rate on clients' debit balances resulting from margin buying.

Margin refers to the portion of the total cost of the security that is paid for by the investor. A 65 percent margin requirement means that the investor must deposit cash (or securities with loan value) equal to 65 percent of the purchase price. If $10,000 in securities were purchased on 65 percent margin, the situation would be:

Market value	$10,000
Debit balance	3,500
Equity	$ 6,500

The equity of $6,500 is derived from the payment in cash of $6,500 to effect the transaction. The $3,500 debit is the difference between the cash payment and the total purchase price of the securities acquired.

Margin requirements—for initial purchases—are established by the Federal Reserve Board of Governors. These are the minimum requirements. Either the Exchange or member firms may have more restrictive rules than the Federal Reserve—but not less restrictive.

Federal initial requirements differ as the Federal Reserve varies requirements as a tool in regulating the economy. The margin requirements also vary according to the type of security being purchased and the account in which such security is purchased. In April 1974 such Federal Margin requirements were as shown in table 7-1.

Rather than use cash, an investor may effect purchases

TABLE 7-1

Margin Initial and Maintenance Requirements

Type of Account	Type of Security	Federal Initial Requirement, Percent	NYSE Minimum Maintenance Requirement
General margin	Listed stocks—NYSE & ASE—approved OTC, & regional exchanges	50	25%
Short sales	All securities other than exempt	50	30% or more depending on price
Exempt:	U.S. treasuries/government agencies	10	5% of principal
	Municipals	25	15% of principal or 25% of market value whichever is lower
	GNMA	25	5% of principal
	FNMA common	55	25%
	FNMA convertible bonds	50	25%
Special subscription	All marginable stocks or bonds	30	25%
Convertible bonds	Listed	50	25%
Nonconvertible bonds	Listed	30	25%
General margin	Call, put, and straddle options long in account	100	100%
	Exercise of a call: exercise call and sell stock short on same day	None	None
	Exercise call and sell stock long on the same day	None	None
	Exercise of a put: exercise put and buy the stock on the same day	None	None

and satisfy the federal initial margin requirements by depositing securities whose "loan value" meets the applicable margin requirement. The loan value of a security is equal to 100 percent less the amount of the margin requirement. For example, for listed stocks the loan value is 100 percent less 50 percent, or 50 percent; for nonconvertible bonds, 100 percent less 30 percent, or 70 percent; for convertible bonds, 100 percent less 50 percent, or 50 percent.

Thus, if an investor buys $10,000 of a listed marginable stock, with 50 percent margin requirement, how much additional common stock collateral must he deposit to his margin account, if he wishes to use no cash? Purchase, $10,000; margin required, $5,000.

$$\text{(The additional stock)} \times 50\% = \$5,000$$

$$\frac{\$5,000}{.50} = \$10,000$$

Then $10,000 additional stock would be required. The position of the account would then be:

Market value	$20,000
Debit	10,000
Equity	$10,000

At this moment the equity ($10,000), is 50 percent of the total market value ($20,000) and the federal initial margin requirements have been satisfied.

In the event that a decline in the market value of the account occurs, the market value and equity would reduce by equal amounts. Declines beyond a certain point would cause a "call" for additional collateral to be made based on New York Stock Exchange or brokerage firm "house" maintenance rules. The New York Stock Exchange minimum maintenance requirement is that equity must be a prescribed percentage of the account's market value, in the percentages as shown in the preceding table. If a client fails promptly to deposit cash or additional collateral in the event of a demand for it, the member firm is obliged to sell all or a part of the investor's margined securities to put the account in a proper position.

An account which has a greater equity than is required by federal initial margin regulations is said to have *excess*. Excess refers to equity which is in excess of the amount required. Excess divided by the federal initial margin percentage (e.g., 65 percent) determines the maximum amount of that account's *buying power*, the amount of additional securities that the account may purchase without using any additional cash. Assume market value is $150,000, and debit is $20,000. Then the equity in the account is $130,000. The requirement is 65 percent times the market value of $150,000; thus the requirement is $97,500. The actual equity of $130,000 is $32,500 in excess of the required amount. The excess of $32,500 divided by the 65 percent requirement provides buying power of $50,000. If the full buying power of $50,000 is used to purchase additional securities on margin without utilizing any cash, the account would now have a total market value of $200,000; the debit would now be $70,000; and the equity remains unchanged at $130,000. The equity now represents exactly 65 percent of the market value and there is no longer any excess or buying power. Should the market value now decline, the account is termed *"restricted."*

Buying power can originate in other ways including, but not limited to, the receipt in the account of dividends, interest, additional cash deposits, and unrealized profits on short positions. If an account has no "excess" it is possible that neither cash nor securities could be withdrawn from the account. On the other hand, there may be no excess and it may be allowable to withdraw some cash or securities from the account. The rules and regulations involved are complex and are beyond the scope of this book. The description above is merely a brief introduction to the main points involving margin and margin accounts.

Minimum Margin Account Deposit. In addition to the applicable margin rate, it is important to note that the New York Stock Exchange requires a minimum equity to open a margin account of $2,000. This $2,000 requirement may be met by the deposit of either cash, loan value of marginable securities, or a combination of both. The one exception where $2,000 is not required to open or maintain a margin account is when the purchase price is less than $2,000 and the stock is paid for in full. For example, it is permissible to open a margin account and effect a purchase therein of 100 shares of a $14 stock, provided that the entire purchase price is paid in full.

A member firm shall not permit a customer to make a practice of effecting transactions requiring margin and then either: (a) deferring the furnishing of margin beyond the time when such transactions would ordinarily be settled or cleared, or (b) meeting such demand for margin by the liquidation of the same or other commitments in his account (where such sale occurs on a day subsequent to the margin purchase).

Every member firm must report to the exchange every instance in which a customer made a purchase requiring margin and met the requirement by liquidation.

Payment for securities purchased in a margin account is governed by Regulation T of the Federal Reserve Board, which provides that payment must be made "as promptly as possible and in any event before the expiration of five full business days following the date of such transaction...." If payment is not received as specified above, the brokerage firm may sell sufficient securities from the margin account to meet the required initial margin. In exceptional cases, the five-day period may be extended for one or more limited periods. The broker does not have the authority to grant such extensions. Approval must be given by a committee of the particular exchange or by the NASD.

Let us now examine the effects of the rules regarding margin on two types of activity involving options: (1) buying a call option, and (2) buying a stock and simultaneously selling a call.

Buying an Option. When one purchases a call option the transaction is effected in a margin account. However, options have no loan value and must be paid for in full either with cash or by deposit in the margin account of other marginable securities with loan value at least equal to the cost of the acquired call. For example, an investor buys a six-month-ten-day call on Extendicare[1] for a premium including tax and brokerage charges of $275. The $275 must be paid in full usually by the next business day following the date of trade. Settlement date is usually the next business day for the purchase of options and similarly the seller of the option normally receives his premium on the next business day.

Buying a Stock and Selling an Option. In this instance there is no margin requirement associated with the sale of the call option. However, the usual margin requirements prevail with respect to purchase of the underlying stock.

We shall consider later the margin requirements with respect to the sale of a "naked" call, that is, the sale of a call option when the investor does not own or simultaneously purchase the requisite number of shares of the optioned stock.

If the margin requirement for a listed common stock is 65 percent at the moment of execution of a purchase of 100 shares of Procter and Gamble at 100, and a call is sold simultaneously for one year for a net premium of $2,000, the margin requirement would be established as follows:

Purchase 100 shares of PG at 100	$10,000
Brokerage cost to buy stock	65
Total gross purchase cost	10,065
Margin requirement ($10,065 at 65%)	6,542.25
Less: premium income received	2,000.00
Actual required cash outlay	$ 4,542.25

[1] Extendicare has changed its name to Humana.

Now, let us consider the magnifying effect (leverage) that results from the use of credit in a margin account. The following actual transactions negotiated by the author on August 9, 1972, involved the purchase of 500 shares of Kingsford (which later merged into Clorox) at a price of 13⅞ per share. Simultaneously, five 65-day call options were sold on the 500 shares with a 13⅞ striking price for a net premium to the option seller of $150 per option, for a total of $750. Providing the options are exercised, the annualized percentage rate of return from this transaction for the option seller was 45.37 percent if full cash was used, and 84.18 percent if one used the maximum allowable margin. The actual computation is shown in figure 7-1.

The "customer's agreement and lending agreement" is a rather one-sided affair. This agreement, which every margin account holder is required to sign by members of the New York Stock Exchange, is reproduced as Appendix A to this chapter. The following points are to be noted:

1. The agreement pertains to all accounts of the customer, not just the margin account.
2. It gives the broker a lien on all property of the customer in the possession of the broker.
3. It allows the broker to lend (e.g., to a bank) all the customer's securities.
4. It requires the customer to pay his debit balance on demand.
5. It allows the broker to sell at his discretion, when the broker deems it desirable, any of the customer's securities.

Even more abhorrent than the above agreement is the "option margin agreement" required by some New York Stock Exchange firms. It is reproduced as Appendix B to this chapter. This agreement provides in part: The broker is not liable except for *gross* negligence or *willful* misconduct. Fortunately, not all brokers are so bold as to foist the latter agreement on their public customers.

FIGURE 7-1

CASH TRANSACTION on _August 9, 1972_

Transaction:
 Buy _500_ shares _Kingsford_ @$13⅞
 and sell _5_ call option(s) (duration _65_ days) for a premium of $ _750.00_
  (options exercisable at 13⅞ per share)

Cost price of _500_ shares of stock ·	$ _6,937.50_
Plus: Brokerage cost to buy above stock ·	$ _114.44_
Gross cash investment ·	$ _7,051.94_
Less: Premium received from sale of options, net · · · · · · · · · · · ·	$ (_750.00_)
Investor's <u>cash outlay,</u> without using margin · · · · · · · · · · · · · · · · · ·	$ _6,301.94_

Return on Investment without Margin:
 Net premium income · $ _750.00_
  Less: Eventual brokerage expense, N.Y. nonresident transfer tax,
   SEC fee to sell shares when stock is sold or "called away"
    To buy · $ (_114.44_)
    To sell · $ (_126.76_)
 PROFIT · $ _508.80_

$$\% \text{ Profit} = \frac{\text{Profit (\$ } 508.80 \text{)} \times (5.62)^\dagger}{\text{Cash Outlay (\$} 6,301.94)} = 45.37 \%$$

MARGIN TRANSACTION on _August 9, 1972_

Transaction:
 Buy _500_ shares _Kingsford_ @ _13⅞_

and sell _5_ call option(s)*(duration _65_ days) for a premium of	$ _750.00_
Cost price of _500_ shares of stock. ·	$ _6,937.50_
Plus: Brokerage cost to buy above stock · · · · · · · · · · · · · · · · · · ·	$ _114.44_
Gross investment cost (GIC) ·	$ _7,051.94_
% Minimum cash (or loan value) required (MCR) _@ 55%_ · · · · · · ·	$ _3,878.56_
Less: Premium received from sale of options, net · · · · · · · · · · · · ·	$ (_750.00_)
Investor's <u>cash outlay,</u> using maximum margin* · · · · · · · · · · · · · · · ·	$ _3,128.56_

Return on Investment with Margin:
 Net premium income. · $ _750.00_
  Less: Eventual brokerage expense, N.Y. nonresident transfer tax,
   SEC fee to sell shares when stock is sold or "called away"
    To buy · $ (_114.44_)
    To sell · $ (_126.76_)
   Interest of about _7%_ for _65_ days on _70.52_ (GIC)
   less $ _3,879_ (MCR); _i.e., $ 3173_ · · · · · · · · · · · · · · $ (_40.10_)
 PROFIT · $ _468.70_

$$\% \text{ Profit} = \frac{\text{Profit (\$ } 468.70 \text{)} \times (5.62)^\dagger}{\text{Cash Outlay (\$ } 3129.00)} = 84.18 \%$$

* Exercisible at 13 7/8.
† 5.62 = 365 days divided by 65 days.

Naked Options. A speculator may sell a call option without owning or purchasing the underlying security at the time of the transaction. These situations are termed "naked" or "unhedged." The minimum margin requirement of the New York Stock Exchange is 30 percent of the option price less the premium received from writing the call.[2] For example, a writer sells a call on Pet, Inc., exercisable at 50, and receives a premium of $700. The market value of the shares under option is $5,000. Thirty percent of $5,000 is $1,500, which is reduced by the $700 premium to the minimum margin amount of $800. However, in the case of this sale of a naked option, if the stock rises, additional funds may be required. The additional funds that may be required are through a process known as "marking to the market." Marks to the market are for 100 percent of the adverse price movement of the security. The following example illustrates margin requirements for naked options.

Investor sells a naked call on 100 shares of Pet at 50. The initial minimum margin requirement is 30 percent times 5,000 or $1,500. Pet increases to 60; the "mark-to-market" additional margin requirement is the increase to $6,000 over the striking price of $5,000—a mark-to-market requirement of $1,000.

Summary. It is important that option writers have a sound understanding of the mechanics of margin accounts. Securities deposited in a margin account, in certain adverse circumstances, may not be withdrawn while the margin account is in a debit position. If securities in a margin account are sold, pursuant to Regulation T, the investor is only guaranteed that he may withdraw 30 percent of the sales proceeds. On the other hand, the use of margin provides substantial leverage to investors because it lessens their cash outlay, and thus the rate of profit or loss is magnified when compared to using full cash. Many New

---

[2] This presumes that the premium is deposited to the option writer's margin account.

York Stock Exchange and NASD firms do not follow the *minimum* margin requirements, as set forth in NYSE or NASD rules, and impose more stringent requirements. It is important that option investors carefully ascertain the requirements of the particular firms where business is to be transacted.

APPENDIX A

1. I agree as follows with respect to all of my accounts, in which I have an interest alone or with others, which I have opened or open in the future, with you for the purchase and sale of securities and commodities:

2 I am of full age and represent that I am not an employee of any exchange or of a Member Firm of any Exchange or the NASD, or of a bank, trust company, or insurance company and that I will promptly notify you if I become so employed.

3. All transactions for my account shall be subject to the constitution, rules, regulations, customs and usages, as the same may be constituted from time to time, of the exchange or market (and its clearing house, if any) where executed.

4. Any and all credit balances, securities, commodities or contracts relating thereto, and all other property of whatsoever kind belonging to me or in which I may have an interest held by you or carried for my accounts shall be subject to a general lien for the discharge of my obligations to you (including unmatured and contingent obligations) however arising and without regard to whether or not you have made advances with respect to such property and without notice to me may be carried in your general loans and all securities may be pledged, repledged, hypothecated or re-hypothecated, separately or in common with other securities or any other property, for the sum due to you thereon or for a greater sum and without retaining in your possession and control for delivery a like amount of similar securities or other property. At any time and from time to time you may, in your discretion, without notice to me, apply and/or transfer any securities, commodities, contracts relating thereto, cash or any other property therein, interchangeably between any of my accounts, whether individual or joint or from any of my accounts to any account guaranteed by me You are specifically authorized to transfer to my cash account on the settlement day following a purchase made in that account, excess funds available in any of my other accounts, including but not limited to any free balances in any margin account or in any non-regulated commodities account, sufficient to make full payment of this cash purchase. I agree that any debit occurring in any of my accounts may be transferred by you at your option to my margin account.

5. I will maintain such margins as you may in your discretion require from time to time and will pay on demand any debit balance owing with respect to any of my accounts. Whenever in your discretion you deem it desirable for your protection, (and without the necessity of a margin call) including but not limited to an instance where a petition in bankruptcy or for the appointment of a receiver is filed by or against me, or an attachment is levied against my account, or in the event of notice of my death or incapacity, or in compliance with the orders of any Exchange, you may, without prior demand, tender, and without any notice of the time or place of sale, all of which are expressly waived, sell any or all securities, or commodities or contracts relating thereto which may be in your possession, or which you may be carrying for me, or buy any securities, or commodities or contracts relating thereto of which my account or accounts may be short, in order to close out in whole or in part any commitment in my behalf or you may place stop orders with respects to such securities or commodities and such sale or purchase may be made at your discretion on any Exchange or other market where such business is then transacted, or at public auction or private sale, with or without advertising and no demands, calls, tenders or notices which you may make or give in any one or more instances shall invalidate the aforesaid waivers on my part. You shall have the right to purchase for your own account any or all of the aforesaid property at any such sale, discharged of any right of redemption, which is hereby waived.

6. All orders for the purchase or sale of commodities for future delivery may be closed out by you as and when authorized or required by the Exchange where made. Against a "long" position in any commodity contract, prior to maturity thereof, and at least five business days before the first notice day of the delivery month, I will give instructions to liquidate, or place you in sufficient funds to take delivery; and in default thereof, or in the event such liquidating instructions cannot be executed under prevailing conditions, you may, without notice or demand, close out the contracts or take delivery and dispose of the commodity upon any terms and by any method which may be feasible. Against a "short" position in any commodity contract, prior to maturity thereof, and at least five business days before the last trading day of the delivery month, I will give you instructions to cover, or furnish you wih all necessary delivery documents; and in default thereof, you may without demand or notice, cover the contracts, or if orders to buy in such contracts cannot be executed under prevailing conditions, you may procure the actual commodity and make delivery thereof upon any terms and by any method which may be feasible.

7. All transactions in any of my accounts are to be paid for or required margin deposited no later than 2:00 p.m. on the settlement date.

8. I agree to pay interest and service charges upon my accounts monthly at the prevailing rate as determined by you.

9. I agree that, in giving orders to sell, all "short" sale orders will be designated as "short" and all "long" sale orders will be designated as "long" and that the designation of a sell order as "long" is a representation on my part that I own the security and, if the security is not in your possession that it is not then possible to deliver the security to you forthwith and I will deliver it on or before the settlement date.

10. Reports of the execution of orders and statements of my account shall be conclusive if not objected to in writing within five days and ten days, respectively, after transmittal to me by mail or otherwise.

11. All communications including margin calls may be sent to me at my address given you, or at such other address as I may hereafter give you in writing, and all communications so sent, whether in writing or otherwise, shall be deemed given to me personally, whether actually received or not.

12. No waiver of any provision of this agreement shall be deemed a waiver of any other provision, nor a continuing waiver of the provision or provisions so waived.

13. I understand that no provision of this agreement can be amended or waived except in writing signed by an officer of your Company, and that this agreement shall continue in force until its termination by me is acknowledged in writing by an officer of your Company; or until written notice of termination by you shall have been mailed to me at my address last given you.

14. This contract shall be governed by the laws of the State of New York, and shall inure to the benefit of your successors and assigns, and shall be binding on the undersigned, his heirs, executors, administrators and assigns. Any controversy arising out of or relating to my account, to transactions with or for me or to this agreement or the breach thereof, shall be settled by arbitration in accordance with the rules then obtaining of either the American Arbitration Association or the Board of Governors of the New York Stock Exchange as I may elect, except that any controversy arising out of or relating to transactions in commodities or contracts relating thereto, whether executed or to be executed within or outside of the United States shall be settled by arbitration in accordance with the rules then obtaining of the Exchange (if any) where the transaction took place, if within the United States, and provided such Exchange has arbitration facilities or under the rules of the American Arbitration Association as I may elect. If I do not make such election by registered mail addressed to you at your main office within five days after demand by you that I make such election, then you may make such election. Notice preliminary to, in conjunction with, or incident to such arbitration proceeding, may be sent to me by mail and personal service is hereby waived. Judgment upon any award rendered by the arbitrators may be entered in any court having jurisdiction thereof, without notice to me.

15. If any provision hereof is or at any time should become inconsistent with any present or future law, rule or regulation of any securities or commodities exchange or of any sovereign government or a regulatory body thereof and if any of these bodies have jurisdiction over the subject matter of this agreement, said provision shall be deemed to be superseded or modified to conform to such law, rule or regulation, but in all other respects this agreement shall continue and remain in full force and effect.

DATE_____CUSTOMER'S SIGNATURE _____   _____

SIGN
.N
BOTH
PLACES

Option Margin Agreement

Date _____
TY-89107-50

_____ & Co.

Dear Sirs:

This letter is written to you in connection with puts and/or calls which you may handle, purchase and/or endorse for my accounts.

We agree that you shall not be liable in connection with the execution, handling, purchasing, exercising and/or endorsing of puts and/or calls for my account, except for gross negligence or willful misconduct on your part.

Supplementing the terms and conditions of your margin agreement, which I have signed and hereby confirm in the event I do not meet your margin calls promptly, you are authorized in your sole discretion, and without notification to me, to take any and all steps necessary to protect yourselves in connection with put and/or call transactions made for my account, including the right to buy and/or sell short, or short exempt, for my account and risk any part or all of the shares represented by options endorsed by you for my account, or to buy for my account and risk any puts and/or calls as you may deem necessary to fully protect yourselves.

We further agree that any and all expenses incurred by you in this connection will be reimbursed by me.

The foregoing provisions and the provisions hereinafter stated in this letter shall apply to all puts and/or calls which you may have executed, purchased and/or handled for my account and also shall apply to all puts and/or calls which you may hereafter purchase, handle and/or execute for my account.

In the event of any dispute between us and/or claim by

me and/or claim by you on account of the purchase, handling, execution and/or endorsement of puts and/or calls for my account, the same shall be arbitrated before the Arbitration Committee of the New York Stock Exchange and in accordance with the rules of such Committee.

Very truly yours

_____

_____

a higher interest yield than he would receive in common stock dividends. Also, the convertible bond may have greater resistance to a downturn than has common stock.

It is important to note the particular circumstances that should exist before one writes a call option against a convertible bond holding. These are: (1) The bond should be selling at or very near to its conversion worth in the underlying common stock, and (2) the common stock should seem to have reasonably small downside risk. In this situation the convertible bond price should move in correlation with the common stock as the common stock rises and the bond should have somewhat more resistance to decline than the common stock.

On December 5, 1973, a call option was sought on MGIC Corporation. The call premium offered to the seller was $937.50 for a six-month-ten-day period. The common stock price was $87 and the convertible bond price was $1,310 per bond. Each bond was convertible into 14.92 shares of common stock. At least seven bonds were needed to provide conversion rights into not less than 100 shares of common stock (100 divided by 14.92 shares per bond equals 6.7 bonds). The common stock value of bonds was $87.80 per share ($1,310 purchase price of one bond divided by 14.92 shares of common stock into which a bond is convertible). Since the market price of the common stock was 87, the bonds were selling very close to parity—one of the two prerequisites for this venture. A comparison follows of the alternatives, i.e., writing the option against (a) common stock acquired for that purpose and (b) convertible bonds. Initial margin requirements at that time were 50 percent for the convertibles and 65 percent for common stock. Interest charged by the brokerage firm on debit balances was 6.5 percent. My client (not I) was convinced that MGIC was an excellent growth security with strong institutional support, and he was not concerned that the stock was then selling for a very high price earnings multiple. He was also satisfied that the premium of $937.50 net was attractive. Thus, the choice was between buying the bonds or buying the common stock. We determined that ownership of the convertibles in the convertible bond margin account would be considered by current New York Stock Exchange rules to fully "hedge or cover" the option sale in the general margin account. (A naked or unhedged sale of a call would entail additional margin requirements.)

There are two other factors to be considered in selling calls against a convertible bond or convertible preferred stock: (a) potential additional margin requirements, and (b) possible need to temporarily sell the stock short. Both such events may occur in the event that the option is actually exercised and will not arise if the option lapses.

In the event that the option is exercised, immediate delivery must be made of the common stock represented by the exercising of the option. Although instructions are given the same day to convert the bonds to common stock, for a few days at least the account of the option writer will be "long" the bonds and "short" the stock. This situation could cause additional margin requirements to be imposed on the writer.[1] Further, the possibility exists that the option writer's brokerage firm might be unable to arrange the temporary short sale of the stock in order to effect delivery on the day of exercise of the option, in which case the writer would have to buy the requisite shares in order to effect delivery to the buyer of the calls.

Summary. The potential annual profit percentage by writing the option against the common stock is 28.51 percent and in the case of the convertible bond is 38.54 percent. The increased rate of return on the bond transaction is due to increased leverage resulting from more

---

[1] Under Regulation T, paragraph 220.3(d)(3), an investor long the bonds and short the stock would not be required to supply additional federal margin. Under NYSE rules, after conversion instructions are issued with respect to the bonds, the margin requirement is 10 percent of the bond's market price and nothing with respect to the short sale which is in process of being covered.

FIGURE 8-1

```
┌──────── ECONOMIC EFFECTS OF BUYING A STOCK AND SELLING AN OPTION ────────
│  MARGIN TRANSACTION on   December 7, 1972
```

Transaction:
Buy __100__ shares __MGIC__ _____ @ _87_
and sell __1__ call option(s) (duration _190_ days) for a premium of $ __937.50__
                    exercisable at $87.00 per share

 Cost price of __100__ shares of stock ....$ __8,700.00__
 Plus: Brokerage cost to buy above stock ....$ ___65.00__

 Gross investment cost (GIC)..........................$ __8,765.00__

 % Minimum cash (or loan value) required (MCR)...............$ __5,655.00__
 Less: Premium received from sale of options, net ....$ (__957.50__)

 Investor's cash outlay, using maximum margin * ....$ __4,717.50__

Return on Investment with Margin:
 Net premium income.....................................$ __937.50__
  Less: Eventual brokerage expense, N.Y. nonresident transfer tax,
  SEC fee to sell shares when stock is sold or "called away":
   To buy...$ (__65.00__)
   To sell...$ (__68.43__)
  Interest of about _6.5_ for _190_ days on __8,765__ ____ (GIC)
  less _5,655_ (MCR); i.e., $3,110 ____..........$ (__105.22__)

PROFIT ....$ __698.85__

$$\% \text{ Profit} = \frac{\text{Profit } (\$\ 698.85\ ) \times (\ 1.92\ )^{\dagger}}{\text{Cash Outlay } (\$\ 4,717.50)} = 28.51\%$$

This is the annualized rate of return at the inception of the transaction. This rate of return will be realized: (a) if the stock rises and the option is exercised, and (b) if the stock remains unchanged and the option expires unexercised. This rate will be higher yet if the stock rises (i.e., slightly) and the option is not exercised. Only in the event that the stock declines below the original purchase price will the rate of return be less. Should the stock decline more than the premium received (less the cost to buy and to sell the stock) a loss would be incurred on the transaction.

When a stock is simply purchased in the conventional manner, the investor only profits if the stock rises. As indicated above, the option-seller (investor) profits handsomely even if the stock remains unchanged, as well as if the stock rises. In addition, the investor can still profit even in the event of a small decline.

Note: If the call option is exercised, then dividends, splits, etc. paid during the option period accrue to the buyer of the option. If the option is not exercised, the option seller retains such dividends. When margin credit is used to the maximum extent, if the market value of the portfolio falls beyond a certain amount, additional collateral or cash could be required, or portfolio securities would have to be sold. Present requirements are that the investor's EQUITY (which is market value less Debit balance) must equal at least 30% of the market value of the portfolio (for stocks with a market value of $10 or higher; for stocks below $10, the requirements are higher). Before any difficulties could be incurred in this respect (margin call) the portfolio could suffer a decline of about 30% from its original cost basis.

* If the investor has Marginable securities in his Account, the loan value is _35_ % of the market value. Such loan value may be utilized in lieu of cash for making a new purchase.

† Conversion factors to an annualized rate of return: $1.92 = 365 \div 190$.

FIGURE 8-2

ECONOMIC EFFECTS OF BUYING A CONVERTIBLE BOND AND SELLING A CALL OPTION

MARGIN TRANSACTION on *December 17, 1972*

Transaction:

Buy __7__ shares *MGIC 4¼'s 1,993* @ *$1,310*

and sell __1__ call option(s) (duration _190_ days) for a premium of .... $ _937.50_
exercisable at $87 per share

Cost price of __7__ bonds	$ 9,170.00
Plus: Brokerage cost to buy above bonds	$ 35.00
Gross investment cost (GIC)	$ 9,205.00
% Minimum cash required (MCR)	$ 4,585.00
Less: Premium received from sale of options, net	$ (937.50)
Investor's cash outlay, using maximum margin	$ 3,647.50

Return on Investment with Margin:

Sales proceeds: *100.00 shares @ 87.00 $ 4.44 shares @ 86⅞*	$ 9,085.72
Less: Gross investment cost (GIC above)	$(9,205.00)
Net premium income	$ 937.50
Excess of bond interest over common stock dividend for 190 day period	$ 152.50
Less: Eventual brokerage expense, N.Y. nonresident transfer tax,	
SEC fee to sell shares when stock is sold or "called away"	
Cost to sell *100 shares*	(68.43)
Cost to sell *4.44 shares*	(14.28)
Interest of about *6.5%* for _190_ days on *$9205* (GIC)	
less *$4585* (MCR) *duly $4620*	$ (156.16)
POTENTIAL PROFIT...............................	$ 731.85

$$\% \text{ Profit} = \frac{\text{Profit (\$ 731.85) x (1.921 Conversion Factor)}}{\text{Cash Outlay (\$3,647.50)}} = 38.54\%$$

liberal margin requirements and from the increased yield that the bond interest provides.

Tax Implications. When the convertible bond is exchanged for common stock the holding period for the newly acquired stock is considered to be backdated to the original acquisition of the bonds. Thus, if the call is exercised, the premium received is added to the sales proceeds from the common stock and receives treatment as long-term capital gain if the bonds were acquired more than six months prior to the date of option exercise. Also, the common stock received on conversion in excess of the 100 shares required to meet the call could be sold at long-term capital gains rates any time more than six months after the bonds were purchased.

9

Record Keeping

In any business activity it is essential to maintain sufficient records to provide necessary data to management for decision making.

Record keeping should also be as simple as possible to produce the information required. The author utilizes five forms, as follows:

1. Percentage return for the sale of a call in a cash transaction.
2. Percentage return in a margin transaction.
3. Master sheet for each brokerage firm account.
4. Stock ledger for each individual security.
5. Balance Sheet and Profit and Loss Statement.

These forms are reproduced as Appendix A through Appendix E at the end of this chapter.

The reader is already familiar with items (1) and (2) above. The potential profit from each transaction must be precisely determined before making a commitment. In particular, all costs associated with the transaction must be determined because the brokerage costs can be a significant part of premium income. Also reproduced as Appendix F are the (January 1974) New York Stock Exchange minimum commission rates, SEC fees, and New York transfer tax levies.

The master sheet serves two prime purposes: (1) it allows the investor to reconcile his records with the monthly statements of his brokerage firm(s); and (2) it provides at one's fingertips all the necessary data for preparing federal tax returns.

The stock ledger facilitates (1) review of one's position in each stock to see if a new option might be sold against an existing holding; (2) review of certain key fundamental and technical factors regarding the stock; (3) recording of new reference data about the stock as they are announced in the press or to stockholders; (4) verification of receipt of dividends, or other distributions; and (5) verification of the striking price adjusted for dividends that serves as the basis for sale when options are exercised and stock is "called away."

The Balance Sheet and Profit and Loss Statement is both a balance sheet and a retained earnings statement. First, the market value, or, where calls have been sold against stocks long, the lower of "market value" or "option price," is determined for each holding. The sum of these amounts (less the market value of securities short) is the present market value of the portfolio. The debit balance is the "negative" balance, if any, of the brokerage account. A continuous record of this balance is maintained on the master sheet.

Subtracting the debit balance from the market value (or adding the credit balance, if such is the case) determines the *investor's equity*. Equity is akin to net worth. It is the amount that could be put in the bank if all the securities were sold and the debit balance (if any) were paid off.

This computation allows the investor to determine the

52

"excess margin requirement," if any, in his account and his buying power, as was discussed in the chapter on margin.

The investor's equity is what his account is worth. To obtain an idea of performance results, it must be related to the sum invested, or cash outlay, which is also continuously recorded on the master sheet. Cash outlay should properly record not only cash but the market value of securities deposited to the investment account, if such securities are used as collateral for borrowing purposes. Cash withdrawn or securities withdrawn from the account should be reflected by negative entries in this account.

The net profit or loss at any time is simply determined as follows:

$$
\begin{array}{ll}
\text{Equity} & \$XXXX \\
\text{Less: cash outlays (net)} & \underline{YYYY} \\
\text{Profit (or loss)} & \overline{(X - Y)}
\end{array}
$$

This profit or loss is an absolute dollar amount rather than a percentage return.

Percentage Return. The percentage return is determined by relating the profit to the cash outlay and the period of time that the cash outlay has been employed.

In addition, the profit (or loss) amount as determined above would have to be adjusted to reflect option premiums collected but not yet fully earned because the options have not yet expired or been exercised. The premium income is a deferred asset until the option is either exercised or expires. This "deferral" aspect of the premium creates certain problems in obtaining a fair appraisal of results. For example, a premium is collected from the sale of a call and shortly thereafter the price of the stock (acquired at the time the call was sold) has declined by $15 per share. The investor's equity reflects the decrease in the value per share and also reflects the premium received from the sale of the call. But if a portion of the premium were removed from equity because the call has not yet expired, it would seem to be inequitable. A very complex mathematical formula is required to determine the actual percentage rate of return based on profit of "$X" and cash outlays of varying sums at varying time intervals. The problem is essentially the same as that required to measure pension fund or trust fund performance. Certain banks and brokerage firms make available computer programs to determine performance at no cost (to substantial potential clients). An approximation of percentage return may be determined by obtaining the average cash outlay over a period of time and by dividing that sum into the profit. An example of computation of percentage return follows:

Date	Cash Outlays
1/1	$2,000
4/1	5,000
7/1	8,000
10/1	5,000

On December 31, of the same year, the balance sheet provided the following information.

Market value of portfolio	$43,000
Less: debit balance at 12/31	20,000
Equity	$23,000
Less: cash outlays	20,000
Profit	$ 3,000

The average cash outlay for the year can be computed as follows:

A	B	
Amount	No. of Months Employed	A × B
$ 2,000	12	$ 24,000
5,000	9	45,000
8,000	6	48,000
5,000	3	15,000
Totals $20,000		$132,000

The approximate *annual percentage profit* can be determined by the following formula: Profit divided by the product of the average cash outlay and the number of years. The average cash outlay per year, in the illustration, is equal to $132,000 divided by 12 months; i.e., $11,000. Profit is $23,000 less $20,000; i.e., $3,000. Hence, the approximate annual percentage profit is:

$$\frac{3,000 \text{ (the profit)}}{11,000 \text{ (the average cash outlay)} \times \text{(the number of years)}} = 27.27\%.$$

Computation of percentage return on investment can be understood more easily by following the computations in the example below.

Date	A Cash Outlay	B No. of Months Invested	A × B
1/1/73	$1,000	48	$ 48,000
1/1/74	1,000	36	36,000
1/1/75	1,000	24	24,000
1/1/76	1,000	12	12,000
Totals	$4,000		$120,000

The average investment is $120,000 divided by 48 months; i.e., $2,500. The equity in the account at December 31, 1976, is $5,000. Profit for the four years is therefore:

$5,000 (equity) − $4,000 (cash outlay) = $1,000 (profit)

$$\frac{\% \text{ return on}}{\text{investment}} = \frac{\text{Profit (\$1,000)}}{\text{Avg. investment (2,500)} \times \text{No. of years (4)}} = \frac{10\%}{\text{per year}}$$

The equity of $5,000 is exactly equal to the results obtained by investing the four $1,000 cash outlays at 10 percent simple[1] interest, as shown below:

$$S = P(1 + rt)$$

where S = the value at the end of the time period (4 years)
P = each investment ($1,000)
r = rate of simple interest per year (10%)
t = time period of the investments (4 years, 3 years, etc.)

$S = 1,000 \ [1 + .1 \ (4)] + [1 + .1 \ (3)] + [1 + .1 \ (2)] + [1 + .1 \ (1)]$
$\quad = 1,000 \ (1.4 + 1.3 + 1.2 + 1.1)$
$\quad = 5,000.$

---

[1] Actual compound results will differ somewhat from the approximate method recommended for use by the investor. The investments at 10 percent compound annual interest would have a value equal to $1,000 \ [(1.1)^4 + (1.1)^3 + (1.1)^2 + (1.1)]$; i.e., $5,105.10. Alternatively, at compound rates the result would be determined as follows:

$$1,000 \ \frac{[(1 + .1)^5 - 1)]}{.1} - 1,000 = 5,105.10$$

Given the $5,000 value, and the dates of the $1,000 cash outlays, to solve for the annual percentage compound return (i), the equation is:

$$5,000 = 1,000 \ [(1 + i)^4 + (1 + i)^3 + (1 + i)^2 + (1 + i)]$$
$$5 = i^4 + 5 i^3 + 10 i^2 + 10 i + 4$$

Since values of i to beyond the 2nd power are extremely small, the i^4 and i^3 terms are disregarded. Hence,

$$0 = 10 i^2 + 10 i - 1.$$

Using the quadratic formula, where $a = 10$; $b = 10$, and $c = -1$; then

$$i = -10 + \sqrt{\frac{10^2 - (4) (10) (-1)}{2(1)}} = \frac{-10 + \sqrt{140}}{20} = \frac{-10 + 11.832}{20}$$

$i = .0916$ or 9.16%

APPENDIX A

```
┌─────────────── ECONOMIC EFFECTS OF BUYING A STOCK AND SELLING AN OPTION ───────────┐
```

CASH TRANSACTION on _____

Transaction:
    Buy_____ shares _____@ _____
    and sell_____ call option(s) (duration_____days) for a premium of $_____
    (Striking price of the option = cost price per share of the stock acquired.)
    Cost price of_____ shares of stock. . . . .$
        Plus: Brokerage cost to buy above stock . . . .$_____
    Gross cash investment . . . .$
        Less: Premium received from sale of options, net . . . .$_____
    Investor's cash outlay, without using margin . . . .$_____

Return on Investment without Margin:
    Net premium income . . . .$_____
        Less: Eventual brokerage expense, N.Y. nonresident transfer tax,
            SEC fee to sell shares when stock is sold or "called away"
            To buy. . . . .$ (   )
            To sell. . . . .$ (   )
        PROFIT . . . .$_____

$$\% \text{ Profit} = \frac{\text{Profit (\$} \qquad) \times (\qquad)^*}{\text{Cash Outlay (\$} \qquad)} = \qquad \%$$

    This is the annualized rate of return at the inception of the transaction. This rate of return will be realized: (a) if the stock rises and the option is exercised, and (b) if the stock remains unchanged and the option expires unexercised. This rate of return will be higher yet if the stock rises (i.e., slightly) and the option is not exercised. Only in the event that the stock declines below the original purchase price will the rate of return be less. Should the stock decline more than the premium received (less the cost to buy and sell the stock) a loss would be incurred on the transaction.

    When a stock is simply purchased in the conventional manner, the investor only profits if the stock rises. As indicated above, the option-seller (investor) profits handsomely even if the stock remains unchanged, as well as if the stock rises. In addition, the investor can still profit even in the event of a small decline.

───────────────

* Conversion factors to an annualized rate of return:

Option Period	Conversion Factor
6 months, 10 days	2
95 days	3.84
65 days	5.62
35 days	10.43

Note: If the call option is exercised, then dividends, splits, etc. paid during the option period accrue to the buyer of the option. If the option is not exercised, the option seller retains such dividends.

APPENDIX B

ECONOMIC EFFECTS OF BUYING A STOCK AND SELLING AN OPTION USING CREDIT (MARGIN)

MARGIN TRANSACTION on _____

Transaction:

Buy _____ shares _____ @ _____
and sell _____ call option(s) (duration ____ days) for a premium of $ _____
(Striking price of the option = cost price per share of the stock acquired.)
Cost price of _____ shares . . . .$ _____
    Plus: Brokerage cost to buy above stock . . . .$ _____
Gross investment cost (GIC) . . . .$ _____
% Minimum cash (or loan value) required (MCR) . . . .$ _____
    Less: Premium received from sale of options, net . . . .$ _____
Investor's cash outlay, using maximum margin * . . . .$ _____

Return on Investment with Margin:

Net premium income. . . . .$
    Less: Eventual brokerage expense, N.Y. nonresident transfer tax,
        SEC fee to sell shares when stock is sold or "called away"
        To buy. . . . .$ (   )
        To sell. . . . .$ (   )
        Interest of about _____ for _____ days on _____ (GIC)
        less _____ (MCR) . . . .$ (_____)
PROFIT . . . .$

$$\% \text{ Profit} = \frac{\text{Profit (\$} \qquad) \times (\qquad)^\dagger}{\text{Cash Outlay (\$} \qquad)} = \qquad \%$$

This is the annualized rate of return at the inception of the transaction. This rate of return will be realized: (a) if the stock rises and the option is exercised, and (b) if the stock remains unchanged and the option expires unexercised. This rate of return will be higher yet if the stock rises (i.e., slightly) and the option is not exercised. Only in the event that the stock declines below the original purchase price will the rate of return be less. Should the stock decline more than the premium received (less the cost to buy and to sell the stock) a loss would be incurred on the transaction.

When a stock is simply purchased in the conventional manner, the investor only profits if the stock rises. As indicated above, the option-seller (investor) profits handsomely even if the stock remains unchanged, as well as if the stock rises. In addition, the investor can still profit even in the event of a small decline.

Note: If the call option is exercised, then dividends, splits, etc. paid during the option period accrue to to to the buyer of the option. If the option is not exercised, the option seller retains such dividends. When margin credit is used to the maximum extent, if the market value of the portfolio falls beyond a certain amount, additional collateral or cash could be required, or portfolio securities would have to be sold. Present requirements are that the investor's EQUITY (which is market value less Debit balance) must equal at least 30% of the market value of the portfolio (for stocks with a market value of $10 or higher; for stocks below $10, the requirements are higher). Before any difficulties could be incurred in this respect (margin call), the portfolio could suffer a decline of about 30% from its original cost basis.

* If the investor has Marginable securities in his Account, the loan value is normally __‡__ % of the market value. Such loan value may be utilized in lieu of cash for making a new purchase.

† Conversion factors to an annualized rate of return:

Option Period	Conversion Factor
6 months, 10 days	2
95 days	3.84
65 days	5.62
35 days	10.43

‡ Depends on margin regulations: at 12/31/73, 35% for listed common stocks.

APPENDIX C

NAME OF ACCOUNT: L.R. Rosen   A/C NO: ty 89107-2-50   TYPE A/C: [x] General Margin / Conv. Bond / Muni. Bond / Other

BROKERAGE FIRM: BROKER'S NAME: BROKER'S PHONE:

Date	Stk.	Quantity	Price S.P.	Price Prem.	Invest. Cost	Deferred Premium Income	Option Expiry	Divid. Income	Interest Charges	Sales Proceeds	Gain or Loss Long Term	Short Term	Other	Cash Outlays (withdrawals)	Brokerage A/C Balance Dr.	Cr.	Bal.
2-28-73	Mattel	400		6	2,467.20										2,467.20		(2,467.20)
2-28-73	Mattel	4 calls	6	1 3/8		550.00	9-10-73									550.00	--0--
2-28-73	Cash deposit													1,917.20		1,917.20	1,917.20
3-23-73	Merrill Lynch	100		17 7/8	1,822.74										1,822.74		(1,822.74)
3-23-73	Merrill Lynch	1 call	17 7/8	2 1/2		250.00	10-03-73									250.00	(1,572.74)
3-30-73	Levitz	100		13 1/2	1,379.55										1,379.55		(2,702.29)
3-30-73	Levitz	1 call	13 1/2	2 1/2		250.00	10-10-73									250.00	(2,055.29)
3-30-73	Cash deposit													647.00		647.00	

APPENDIX D

STOCK LEDGER

Name of Stock: (Mattel, Inc.   )

Indicated Annual Dividend – $ 0.10
Date: Latest Div. (1-19-73) Payment Ex-Date (12-15-72) Amount (0.025)

PE Multiple — High (71 year) (47)   Low (73 year) (20)

Last 2 Years — Price (71 year)   High (52 1/4) (73 year)   Low (71 year) (±6)

Date	No. and Type of Option or No. Shares	Prem. per Sh. Striking Price or Cost per Share	1968	1969	1970	1971	1972	Interim EPS	Share Balance	Cost	Deferred Premium	Option Expiry	Sales Proceeds	Gain (Loss)	Dividend Income
								9 Mos. Oct. 0.39 vs ⟨0.25⟩							
2-28-73	400	6	0.64	0.92	1.11	⟨1.66⟩	Est. 0.30		400	2,467.20					
2-28-73	4 calls	1 3/8 6									550.00	9-10-73			

APPENDIX D *(Continued)*

Name of Stock: (Levitz)

Indicated Annual Dividend – $ 0.00
Date: Latest Div. Payment Ex-Date Amount
(-----) (-----) (-----)

PE Multiple — High (72 year) (81) Low (72 year) (17)

Price (72 year) (60 1/2)

Last 2 Years — High Low (73 year) (± 13)

Date	No. and Type of Option or No. Shares	Prem. per Sh.	Striking Price or Cost per Share	1968	1969	1970	1971	1972	Interim EPS	Share Balance	Cost	Deferred Premium	Option Expiry	Sales Proceeds	Gain (Loss)	Dividend Income
				0.14	0.19	0.29	0.56	Est. 0.75	9 Mos. Oct. 0.46 vs 0.34 1973 Est. 1.20							
3-30-73	100		13 1/2							100	1,379.55					
3-30-73	1 call	2 1/2	13 1/2									250.00	10-10-73			

APPENDIX D (Concluded)

Name of Stock: (Merrill Lynch)

Indicated Annual Dividend – $ 0.56
Date: Latest Div. Payment (2-1-73) Ex-Date (1-22-73) Amount (0.14)

Date	Transaction — No. and Type of Option or No. Shares	Prem. per Sh.	Striking Price or Cost per Share	Price (72 year)	High (46)	Low (24)	1968	1969	1970	1971	1972	Interim EPS	Share Balance	Cost	Deferred Premium	Option Expiry	Sales Proceeds	Gain (Loss)	Dividend Income
3-23-73	100		17 7/8				1.44	0.94	1.28	2.47	Est. 2.98		100.00	1,822.74	250.00	10-03-73			
3-23-73	1 call	2 1/2	17 7/8																

APPENDIX E

BALANCE SHEET & PROFIT & LOSS STATEMENT

DATE OF PREPARATION 3-30-73

MONTH	J	F	M	A	M	J	J	A	S	O	N	D
NO. OF DAYS	31	28	31	30	31	30	31	31	30	31	30	31
CUMUL. NO. OF DAYS	31	59	90	120	151	181	212	243	273	304	334	365

Quantity	Stock	A Market Price	B Option Price	C Lower of Mkt. or Option	D Quantity Times "C"
400	Mattel	6 1/2			2,400.00
4 calls	Mattel exp. 9-10-73		6	6	-0-
100	Merrill-Lynch	18			1,787.50
1 call	Merrill-Lynch exp. 10-3-73		17 7/8	17 7/8	-0-
100	Levitz	13 1/2			1,350.00
1 call	Levitz exp. 10-10-73		13 1/2	13 1/2	-0-

(i) Total of column "D" (lower of mkt. val. or option price) 5,537.50
(ii) Debit balance (from master sheet) .... -(2,055.29)
(iii) Equity (i) less (ii) 3,482.21
(iv) Less: Brokerage cost to sell; 1.8% times amt. in (i) .... -(99.68)
(iv-a) Less: interest: $\underline{2055}$ (debit – ii) × $[\underline{193}$ (days – "L") ÷ 365 days] × 7% interest rate .... -(76.06)
(v) Adjusted net equity 3,306.47
(vi) Cash outlays (total of column 10 – master sheet) .... -(2,564.20)
(vii) Profit (or loss) – (v) less (vi) 742.27
(viii) Average investment ("K" from schedule "X") 2,475.00
(ix) Elapsed time ("J" from schedule "X") 224.00
(x) % RETURN ON CASH OUTLAY =

$$\left[\frac{742.27 \text{ (vii)}}{\text{Profit (vii)}} \div \frac{2475 \text{ (vii)}}{\text{Ave. inv. (viii)}}\right] \times \frac{224 \text{ days (ix)}}{365} = 48.87\%^{\dagger}$$

Schedule "X" – Average Investment (cash outlay)

E Amount of cash outlay*	F Date of outlay*	G Time elapsed from "F" until the later of today or the date on which last option expires	H "E" times "G"
1,917.20	2-28-73	224 days	4,294.53
647.00	3-30-73	193 days	1,248.71

"I" Total of column "H" 5,543.24
"J" Elapsed time (largest no. in col. "G") 224.00
"K" Average investment ("I") ÷ ("J") 2,475.00

"L" days from today until date last option expires (see iv-a) .... $\underline{193}$

* from master sheet
† neglecting dividend & interest income and personal taxes

APPENDIX F

NEW YORK, AMERICAN AND OTHER MAJOR STOCK EXCHANGES

COMMISSION RATES EFFECTIVE SEPTEMBER 25, 1973

THE NON-MEMBER MINIMUM COMMISSION ON STOCKS AND WARRANTS SELLING BELOW $1.00 PER SHARE

The nonmember minimum commission on stocks and warrants below $1.00 per share on that portion of an order involving $300,000 or less, shall be based upon the amount involved in the order and shall not be less than:

Amount Involved In The Order	Minimum Commission
$0-but under $1,000	8.4% of money involved
$1,000-but under $10,000	5.0% of money involved plus 34.00
$10,000-and above	4.0% of money involved plus $134.00

Plus 10% on orders not exceeding $5,000, and 15% on any order involving an amount in excess of $5,000

Notwithstanding the foregoing, when the amount involved in an order is less than $100.00, the commission shall be as mutually agreed.

SELLING AT $1.00 AND ABOVE

Commissions on stocks selling at $1 per share and above are to be computed on the basis of the amount of money involved in an order. The schedule of rates should be applied to each single order, as defined.

The Constitution sets forth the minimum commission as follows:

On 100 Share Orders and Odd Lot Orders

Money Involved In The Order	Minimum Commission
$ 100-but under $ 800	2.0% plus $ 6.40
$ 800-but under $2,500	1.3% plus $12.00
$2,500-and above	0.9% plus $22.00

Odd Lot-$2 Less

Multiple Round Lot Orders

Money Involved In The Order	Minimum Commission
$ 100-but under $ 2,500	1.3% plus $ 12.00
$ 2,500-but under $ 20,000	0.9% plus $ 22.00
$20,000-but under $ 30,000	0.6% plus $ 82.00
$30,000-to and including $300,000	0.4% plus $142.00

SHARE PRICE	5	10	20	25	30	50	75	100	200	300	500	1000
$1								9.24	18.48	27.72	46.20	92.40
2						7.04	8.14	11.44	22.88	34.32	57.20	107.80
3						8.14	9.79	13.64	27.28	40.92	66.65	119.90
4				7.04	7.48	9.24	11.44	15.84	31.68	47.52	74.80	129.80
5			7.04	7.59	8.14	10.34	13.09	18.04	36.08	54.12	81.95	139.70
6			7.48	8.14	8.80	11.44	14.74	20.24	40.48	58.74	86.90	156.40
7			7.92	8.69	9.46	12.54	16.39	22.44	44.88	63.03	91.85	166.75
8			8.36	9.24	10.12	13.64	18.04	24.64	49.28	67.32	96.80	177.00
9			8.80	9.79	10.78	14.74	19.69	26.07	52.14	70.73	101.75	187.45
10		7.04	9.24	10.34	11.44	15.84	21.34	27.50	55.00	73.70	106.70	197.80
11		7.26	9.68	10.89	12.10	16.94	22.80	28.93	57.86	76.67	116.73	208.15
12		7.48	10.12	11.44	12.76	18.04	23.87	30.36	60.72	79.64	121.90	218.50
13		7.70	10.56	11.99	13.42	19.14	24.95	31.79	63.14	82.61	127.08	228.85
14		7.92	11.00	12.54	14.08	20.24	26.02	33.22	65.12	85.58	132.25	239.20
15		8.14	11.44	13.09	14.74	21.34	27.09	34.65	67.10	88.55	137.43	249.55
16		8.36	11.88	13.64	15.40	22.44	28.16	36.08	69.08	91.52	142.60	259.90
17		8.58	12.32	14.19	16.06	23.16	29.24	37.51	71.06	98.79	147.78	270.25
18		8.80	12.76	14.74	16.72	23.87	30.31	38.94	73.04	101.89	152.95	280.60
19		9.02	13.20	15.29	17.38	24.59	31.38	40.37	75.02	105.00	158.13	290.95
20	7.04	9.24	13.64	15.84	18.04	25.30	32.45	41.80	77.00	108.10	163.30	301.30
21	7.15	9.46	14.08	16.39	18.70	26.02	33.53	43.23	78.98	111.21	168.48	308.20
22	7.26	9.68	14.52	16.94	19.36	26.73	34.60	44.66	80.96	114.31	173.65	315.10
23	7.37	9.90	14.96	17.49	20.02	27.45	35.67	46.09	82.94	117.42	178.83	322.00
24	7.48	10.12	15.40	18.04	20.68	28.16	36.74	47.52	84.92	120.52	184.00	328.90
25	7.59	10.34	15.84	18.59	21.34	28.88	37.82	48.95	86.90	123.63	189.18	335.80
26	7.70	10.56	16.28	19.14	22.00	29.59	38.89	49.94	92.92	126.73	194.35	342.70
27	7.81	10.78	16.72	19.69	22.58	30.31	39.96	50.93	94.99	129.84	199.53	349.60
28	7.92	11.00	17.16	20.24	23.01	31.02	41.03	51.92	97.06	132.94	204.70	356.50
29	8.03	11.22	17.60	20.79	23.44	31.74	42.11	52.91	99.13	136.05	209.88	363.40
30	8.14	11.44	18.04	21.34	23.87	32.45	43.18	53.90	101.20	139.15	215.05	370.30
31	8.25	11.66	18.48	21.89	24.30	33.17	44.25	54.89	103.27	142.26	220.23	374.90
32	8.36	11.88	18.92	22.44	24.73	33.88	45.32	55.88	105.34	145.36	225.40	379.50
33	8.47	12.10	19.36	22.80	25.16	34.60	46.40	56.87	107.41	148.47	230.58	384.10
34	8.58	12.32	19.80	23.16	25.59	35.31	47.25	57.86	109.48	151.57	235.75	388.70
35	8.69	12.54	20.24	23.52	26.02	36.03	47.99	58.85	111.55	154.68	240.93	393.30
36	8.80	12.76	20.68	23.87	26.44	36.74	48.73	59.84	113.62	157.78	246.10	397.90
37	8.91	12.98	21.12	24.23	26.87	37.46	49.48	60.83	115.69	160.89	251.28	402.50
38	9.02	13.20	21.56	24.59	27.30	38.17	50.22	61.82	117.76	163.99	256.45	407.10
39	9.13	13.42	22.00	24.95	27.73	38.89	50.96	62.81	119.83	167.10	261.63	411.70
40	9.24	13.64	22.44	25.30	28.16	39.60	51.70	63.80	121.90	170.20	266.80	416.30
41	9.35	13.86	22.73	25.66	28.59	40.32	52.45	64.79	123.97	173.30	270.25	420.90
42	9.46	14.08	23.01	26.02	29.02	41.03	53.19	65.78	126.04	176.41	273.70	425.50
43	9.57	14.30	23.30	26.38	29.45	41.75	53.93	66.77	128.11	179.52	277.15	430.10
44	9.68	14.52	23.58	26.73	29.88	42.46	54.67	67.76	130.18	182.62	280.60	434.70
45	9.79	14.74	23.87	27.09	30.31	43.18	55.42	68.75	132.25	185.73	284.05	439.30
46	9.90	14.96	24.16	27.45	30.73	43.89	56.16	69.74	134.32	188.83	287.50	443.90
47	10.01	15.18	24.44	27.81	31.16	44.61	56.90	70.73	136.39	191.94	290.95	448.50
48	10.12	15.40	24.73	28.16	31.59	45.32	57.64	71.50	138.46	195.04	294.40	453.10
49	10.23	15.62	25.01	28.52	32.02	46.04	58.39	71.59	140.53	198.15	297.85	457.70
50	10.34	15.84	25.30	28.88	32.45	46.75	59.13	71.50	142.60	201.25	301.30	462.30

51	10.45	16.06	25.59	29.24	32.88	47.25	59.87	74.75	144.67	204.35	304.75	466.90
52	10.56	16.28	25.87	29.59	33.31	47.74	60.61	74.75	146.74	207.46	308.20	471.50
53	10.67	16.50	26.16	29.95	33.74	48.24	61.36	74.75	148.81	210.56	311.65	476.10
54	10.78	16.72	26.44	30.31	34.17	48.73	62.10	74.75	149.50	213.67	315.10	480.70
55	10.89	16.94	26.73	30.67	34.60	49.23	62.84	74.75	149.50	216.78	318.55	485.30
56	11.00	17.16	27.02	31.02	35.02	49.72	63.58	74.75	149.50	219.88	322.00	489.90
57	11.11	17.38	27.30	31.38	35.45	50.22	64.33	74.75	149.50	222.99	325.45	494.50
58	11.22	17.60	27.59	31.74	35.88	50.71	65.07	74.75	149.50	224.25	328.90	499.10
59	11.33	17.82	27.87	32.10	36.31	51.21	65.81	74.75	149.50	224.25	332.35	503.70
60	11.44	18.04	28.16	32.45	36.74	51.70	66.72	74.75	149.50	224.25	335.80	508.30
61	11.55	18.26	28.45	32.81	37.17	52.20	67.30	74.75	149.50	224.25	338.10	512.90
62	11.66	18.48	28.73	33.17	37.60	52.69	68.04	74.75	149.50	224.25	340.40	517.50
63	11.77	18.70	29.02	33.53	38.03	53.19	68.78	74.75	149.50	224.25	342.70	522.10
64	11.88	18.92	29.30	33.88	38.46	53.68	69.52	74.75	149.50	224.25	345.00	526.70
65	11.99	19.14	29.59	34.24	38.89	54.18	70.27	74.75	149.50	224.25	347.30	531.30
66	12.10	19.36	29.88	34.60	39.31	54.67	71.01	74.75	149.50	224.25	349.60	535.90
67	12.21	19.58	30.16	34.96	39.74	55.17	74.75	74.75	149.50	224.25	351.90	540.50
68	12.32	19.80	30.45	35.31	40.17	55.66	74.75	74.75	149.50	224.25	354.20	545.10
69	12.43	20.02	30.73	35.67	40.60	56.16	74.75	74.75	149.50	224.25	356.50	549.70
70	12.54	20.24	31.02	36.03	41.03	56.65	74.75	74.75	149.50	224.25	358.80	554.30
71	12.65	20.46	31.31	36.39	41.46	57.15	74.75	74.75	149.50	224.25	361.10	558.90
72	12.76	20.68	31.59	36.74	41.89	57.64	74.75	74.75	149.50	224.25	363.40	563.50
73	12.87	20.90	31.88	37.10	42.32	58.14	74.75	74.75	149.50	224.25	365.70	568.10
74	12.98	21.12	32.16	37.46	42.75	58.63	74.75	74.75	149.50	224.25	368.00	572.70
75	13.09	21.34	32.45	37.82	43.18	59.13	74.75	74.75	149.50	224.25	370.30	577.30
76	13.20	21.56	32.74	38.17	43.60	59.62	74.75	74.75	149.50	224.25	372.60	581.90
77	13.31	21.78	33.02	38.53	44.03	60.12	74.75	74.75	149.50	224.25	373.75	586.50
78	13.42	22.00	33.31	38.89	44.46	60.61	74.75	74.75	149.50	224.25	373.75	591.10
79	13.53	22.22	33.59	39.25	44.89	61.11	74.75	74.75	149.50	224.25	373.75	595.70
80	13.64	22.44	33.88	39.60	45.32	61.60	74.75	74.75	149.50	224.25	373.75	600.30
81	13.75	22.58	34.17	39.96	45.75	62.10	74.75	74.75	149.50	224.25	373.75	604.90
82	13.86	22.73	34.45	40.32	46.18	62.59	74.75	74.75	149.50	224.25	373.75	609.50
83	13.97	22.87	34.74	40.68	46.61	63.09	74.75	74.75	149.50	224.25	373.75	614.10
84	14.08	23.01	35.02	41.03	46.95	63.58	74.75	74.75	149.50	224.25	373.75	618.70
85	14.19	23.16	35.31	41.39	47.25	64.08	74.75	74.75	149.50	224.25	373.75	623.30
86	14.30	23.30	35.60	41.75	47.54	64.57	74.75	74.75	149.50	224.25	373.75	627.90
87	14.41	23.44	35.88	42.11	47.84	65.07	74.75	74.75	149.50	224.25	373.75	632.50
88	14.52	23.58	36.17	42.46	48.14	65.56	74.75	74.75	149.50	224.25	373.75	637.10
89	14.63	23.73	36.45	42.82	48.43	66.06	74.75	74.75	149.50	224.25	373.75	641.70
90	14.74	23.87	36.74	43.18	48.73	66.55	74.75	74.75	149.50	224.25	373.75	646.30
91	14.85	24.01	37.03	43.54	49.03	67.05	74.75	74.75	149.50	224.25	373.75	650.90
92	14.96	24.16	37.31	43.89	49.32	67.54	74.75	74.75	149.50	224.25	373.75	655.50
93	15.07	24.30	37.60	44.25	49.62	68.04	74.75	74.75	149.50	224.25	373.75	660.10
94	15.18	24.42	37.88	44.61	49.92	68.53	74.75	74.75	149.50	224.25	373.75	664.70
95	15.29	24.59	38.17	44.97	50.22	69.03	74.75	74.75	149.50	224.25	373.75	669.30
96	15.40	24.73	38.46	45.32	50.51	69.52	74.75	74.75	149.50	224.25	373.75	673.90
97	15.51	24.87	38.74	45.68	50.81	70.02	74.75	74.75	149.50	224.25	373.75	678.50
98	15.62	25.01	39.03	46.04	51.11	70.51	74.75	74.75	149.50	224.25	373.75	683.10
99	15.73	25.16	39.31	46.40	51.40	71.00	74.75	74.75	149.50	224.25	373.75	687.70
100	15.84	25.30	39.60	46.75	51.70	71.50	74.75	74.75	149.50	224.25	373.75	692.30

Plus (for Each Round Lot)

First to tenth round lot .... $6 per round lot

Eleventh round lot and above .... $4 per round lot

Plus On any order involving an amount not in excess of $5,000, the commission computed in accordance with the foregoing provisions shall be increased by 10%, and on any order involving an amount in excess of $5,000, the commission computed in accordance with such provisions shall be increased by 15%.

The minimum commission on a 100 share order or an odd lot order need not be more than $71.50/74.75 (based on amount of money involved) The minimum commission per round lot within a multiple round lot order is not to exceed the single round lot commission computed in accordance with the rate for 100 share orders.

STOCK TRANSFER TAXES

FEDERAL

Expiration-Security transactions have not been subject to Federal taxes since Dec. 31, 1965.

NEW YORK STATE

A tax imposed by the state when a security is sold or transferred from one person to another. The tax is paid by the seller. Sales by out-of-state residents not employed in New York are taxed at reduced rates as indicated in second table below.

Shares selling at	TAX Per Sh.	SALES BY NON RESIDENTS TAX Per Sh.
Less than $5	1¼¢	0.625
$5 but less than $10	2½¢	1.25
$10 but less than $20	3¾¢	1.875
$20 or more	5¢	2.5

MAXIMUM tax on a 'single Taxable sale' is $350.

The rate on transfers not involving a sale is 2½¢ a share.

New York State does not impose a transfer tax on sales or transfers of rights to subscribe or warrants.

FLORIDA

15¢ per $100 par value (or fraction thereof) regardless of selling price.

15¢ per $100 actual value (or fraction thereof) on no par stock, but not to exceed 15¢ on each share.

S. E. C. FEE-TRANSACTIONS ON ANY REGISTERED EXCHANGE

1¢ for each $500 or fraction thereof of money involved.

10

Stock Market Strategy and Call Options

An investor's investment strategy and the actions he takes with respect to options will vary depending on his assessment of general market conditions, conditions in particular industries, and conditions of individual companies.

Bearish on Market and Bearish on Stock. If an investor thinks the market as a whole is likely to decline (termed "bearish") and also is particularly bearish about ABC Company for either fundamental factors (poor industry prospects, bad management, overcapacity in ABC's industry, inability to meet import competition, market saturation, shrinking profit margins, and so on), or technical factors (flow of funds into ABC stock is exceeded by flow out, stock charts show "head and shoulders" top, or other negative configurations), then the strategy involving call options would be to sell naked calls—i.e., sell call

options without purchasing the stock of ABC Company—
or buy a "put," as described in chapter 14.

Example of Sale of a Naked Call Option. Sell a one-
year call option on ABC exercisable at $50 per share for a
premium of $1,500 net. Potential profit is the premium
of $1,500. Cash outlay: The typical margin requirements
for sale of a naked call at a New York Stock Exchange
member firm are 40 percent (minimum is 30 percent) of
the market value of the stock (even though the stock is
not purchased).

Market value of ABC	$5,000
Margin requirement at 40%	2,000
Less: premium income	(1,500)
Cash outlay	$ 500

The maximum return on this investment is determined as
follows:

$$\frac{\text{Profit potential (\$1,500)}[1]}{\text{Cash outlay (\$500) times years (1)}} = 300\%$$

This 300 percent is the rate of return that is actually
realized if the call option which was sold expires unexercised. Normally, one would expect this rate of return to
be realized if ABC stock stays at $50 or declines.

Risks in the Sale of a Naked Call. The profit potential
is realized if the stock stays the same or declines. The
profit is reduced or eliminated if the ABC shares go up. If
ABC shares rise substantially, a large loss could be incurred.

Example of Loss from the Sale of a Naked Call. ABC
increases to $100 per share (from $50 when the naked call
was sold exercisable at $50) and the call option is exer-
cised by the buyer. The seller of the naked call must either
buy 100 shares of ABC at 100 and immediately sell them
for 50 to the option buyer or simply sell 100 ABC short

---

[1] In addition, interest earned on the margin requirement of $2,000 (if
invested in treasury bills, for example) would add to the profit potential.

(sell borrowed stock in expectation of later buying the stock cheaper at which time the short sale is closed out).

Premium income was $1,500, net. One hundred ABC shares must be purchased at 100, the prevailing market price at the time the option is exercised.

```
Cost of 100 ABC at 100 . . . . . . . . . . . . .   $10,000
Plus: brokerage fees . . . . . . . . . . . . . . . .   $     65
Total cost of 100 shares . . . . . . . . . . . .   $10,065
```

The 100 newly acquired shares are then sold to the option buyer at the striking price of the option, $50 per share.

```
Sales proceeds of 100 ABC at 50 . . . . . . .   $5,000
Less: brokerage . . . . . . . . . . . . . . . . . . .   (65)
Less: SEC fee . . . . . . . . . . . . . . . . . . . .   (0.10)
Less: N.Y. nonresident transfer tax . . . . . .   (3.25)
Net sales proceeds . . . . . . . . . . . . . . . .   $4,931.65
```

The annualized loss on investment from the sale of the naked call is an enormous 726.67 percent, determined as follows:

```
Cost from above of 100 shares . . . . . . . .   $10,065.00
Less: sales proceeds . . . . . . . . . . . . . . .   (4,931.65)
Less: premium from sale of call . . . . . . .   (1,500.00)
Net loss . . . . . . . . . . . . . . . . . . . . . . .   $ 3,633.35
```

$$\% \text{ loss on investment} = \frac{\text{Net loss } (3,633.35)}{\text{Cash outlay (\$500) times years (1)}} = 726.67\%$$

Further, as the stock increased additional margin calls would have been made by the broker for cash or additional marginable collateral.

The upside risk, in the event that the stock increases in price and the option is exercised, may be eliminated or reduced by purchasing ABC stock at a predetermined level; e.g., at 60. A *stop order to buy* could be placed to buy 100 ABC at 60. This order automatically becomes a market order if ABC trades at 60. However, at the moment of purchase, though upside risk is eliminated, downside risk commences. This is true because if ABC declines below 60, there is an unrealized loss on the newly acquired 100 ABC shares. In the securities industry, this type of reversal of risk situation is termed "being whipsawed."

The opinion of the author is that the best procedure is to decide on one's estimate of the situation and then stick with it, unless some basic change occurs from the circumstances that induced the original decision. The only person who is sure to make money on situations of the whipsaw type is the stockbroker.

Bearish on Market and Bullish on a Stock, and Bullish on Market and Bullish on a Stock. In these events, if one feels the outlook for appreciation of ABC stock is greater than the likely decline in the market as a whole, the investment strategy would be to buy ABC and sell a call option, as was described in chapter 1.

Bullish on Market and Bearish on a Stock. If one feels that ABC stock will decline even in moderately or strongly rising market conditions, the strategy would be to sell naked calls (or buy a put) as has been previously discussed.

11

Option Premiums

The premium which an option seller receives from the sale of a call (and the price that a buyer is willing to pay) is dependent upon several factors, as follows:

1. Supply and demand. The more anxious the buyer is to buy, and the smaller the number of potential sellers, the higher the premium.

2. Volatility of the stock. The greater the price range fluctuation of the stock, the higher the option premium and vice versa.

3. Quality of the stock. The higher the quality of the stock, as rated by services such as Moody's and Standard and Poor's Corporation, the lower the option premium, and vice versa.

4. Duration of the option. The longer the time period the higher the premium, and vice versa. However, although the dollar quantity is larger for a longer period, the annualized percentage of premium to value of stock is higher for shorter periods.

Option transactions are executed at prices that reflect actual negotiation between the seller and buyer through the intermediary of a stock broker or put and call broker-dealer, or both. As a result, actual prices at which transactions occur will vary from day to day and cannot be quantified in terms of specific rules.

The author acted as a broker for about 90 option sellers. In an attempt to provide helpful data concerning the relationship between premium, stock price, time, and rating, one of my more active accounts is analyzed in figure 11-1 (pages 74-75). The author believes that this account is representative of the general pattern that exists.

Percentage relationships are expressed in terms of the price of the stock and premium received (adjusted in cases in which the striking price was negotiated at a price different from the cost price of the stock being acquired—at the moment of the trade). These percentages do not represent profits and do not reflect brokerage expenses, taxes, dividend adjustments, and so forth.

Figure 11-1 is a record of 37 actual transactions and represents every option transaction that transpired in the particular account during the period that the author was a stockbroker. The number of transactions is not large enough to consider it a significant sample. However, the author is of the opinion that certain viable observations may be made with respect to the data available.

1. The highest seven percentage premiums were all obtained on transactions that involved either (a) over-the-counter (O-T-C) stocks, or (b) listed stocks, with option durations of 95 days, or less.

O-T-C issues generally command higher premiums than listed stocks. In the event that an option of relatively short duration is not exercised, it may be difficult to sell advantageously a new option on the same stock at the then prevailing market price.

2. The transactions that produced the lowest percentage indication all shared the following characteristics:

(a) The option duration was six months ten days or longer and (b) Standard and Poor's Corporation ranked all the stocks in this category at "B" or higher.

3. The two stocks ranked "A–" or better both commanded low option premiums; one was 37th out of 37; and the other 34th out of 37 in the numerical rankings.

Option premiums are commonly expressed as a percentage of the then current market price of the stock. The table below indicates the approximate range of premium percentages that a writer might expect to receive.

Option Time Period	Risk and Volatility of Stock	Percent Premium to Market Price of Stock
35 days	high	4.8 to 6.6
	low	3.5 to 4.8
65 days	high	6.7 to 10.1
	low	4.4 to 6.7
95 days	high	10 to 14
	low	5.4 to 10
6 months 10 days	high	15 to 25
	low	8 to 15

Premiums are proportionately higher for short-term options because brokerage commissions to purchase and sell the stock involved assume a proportionately larger significance in relation to the premium received. These brokerage costs which serve to reduce the potential profit of the writer remain constant irrespective of the duration of the option.

FIGURE 11-1
Analysis of a Particular Option Account

Date	Name of Stock	S & P Rating*	Option Premium (Col. A) and Cost or Last Trade per Share of Stock (Col. B)												Per Transaction % Indicator‡	Numerical Rank
			35 Days		65 Days		95 Days		193 Days		9 Mo.		1 Year		$\frac{A}{B} \times \frac{365}{\text{No. Days}}$	
			A	B	A	B	A	B	A	B	A	B	A	B		
1972																
7/27	Arctic Enterprises	–							3⅛	24¼					25.76	
7/27	Vornado	B							2⅜	15½					30.64	
8/1	Rapid American	B									2¾	16				32
8/10	Crane	B+							1⅞	16⅞					22.22	33
8/22	Pacific Southwest Airlines	–							2¾	21½					25.58	
9/1	Horizon	–							3¾	26⅛					28.70	
9/5	Kingsford (merged Clorox)	B							2⅜	14⅛					33.62	
9/8	Wickes	A–							2⅞	26¾					21.48	34
9/27	National Homes	–							2	12⅝					31.68	
10/6	Northwest Industries	B							3⅛	29½					21.18	35
10/11	Pacific Southwest Airlines	–							2⅝	20⅛					26.08	
10/12	Horizon	–							2⅝	14½					36.20	
10/20	Prel	–					1½	9½							60.62	4
10/20	Merrill Lynch	–							3	25¼					23.76	
10/27	Gulf & Western Industries	B+							3½	35⅛					19.92	36
10/21	Seaboard World Airline	B							2	12⅛					32.98	
11/3	Kingsford†		1	12½											83.42	1
11/6	National Homes	–							1¾	11¼					31.10	
11/6	Gulf Oil	A+											3	23¼	12.90	37
11/6	Kingsford	B					1.95	11.5							65.12	3
11/9	Mohawk Data	–							2	13⅝					29.34	

Date	Company	Rating													Cost of stock	
12/13	Homestake Mining	B							2 3/4	24					22.90	31
12/14	Viking General	—							2	13 1/4					29.08	
12/18	Mattel	B							2 3/8	14 3/8					33.04	77
12/18	Pepsi Cola Bottling, Wash.	(O-T-CB)							2 3/8	11 3/8					40.42	30
12/19	Homestake Mining	B							2 3/4	24					22.90	
12/20	Merle Norman	—			1.5	15									56.15	5
12/21	Thiokol	—							2 1/4	18 7/8					23.84	
12/27	Arlen Realty & Develop.	B							1 3/4	11 5/8					30.10	
12/29	Arlen Realty & Develop.	B					1.25	12.75							37.65	
1973																
1/2	Schaefer (F & M)	—							1 1/2	9 5/8					31.16	
1/3	Philips Industries	B+							1 11/16	11					30.68	
1/8	Patrick Petroleum	O-T-C—							2 1/8	9 1/4					45.94	6
1/10	Patrick Petroleum	O-T-C—					1 15/16	99 7/8							75.38	2
1/11	Pacific Southwest Airlines	—							2 1/2	19 3/4					25.30	
1/15	Horizon	—							2 1/4	13 1/4					33.96	
1/19	Fuqua Industries	B							2	17					23.52	
	Totals		1	12.5	1.5	15	6.6375	43.63	70.1	517.5	2.75	16	3	23.25		
	Percent premium divided by cost of stock		8%		10%		15.21%		13.53%		17.18%		12.90%			
	Conversion factor to annualize premiums		10.4285		6.0833		3.8421		2.0		1.333		1.0			
	Percent annualized		83.4%		60.83%		58.45%		27.07%		22.91%		12.90%			

$$\left(\frac{\text{Premium} \times \text{conv. factor}}{\text{Cost or last trade}}\right)$$

*Standard & Poor's Corporation ratings are a scoring system based upon earnings and dividend records. Those stocks which are assigned a rating, range from highest (A+) to lowest (C),

†The option sold was a straddle; therefore, only two thirds of the premium is included for the call premium.

‡Excludes brokerage costs, taxes, SEC fees; the data presented above cannot be used to determine portfolio performance results because the date of option exercise, if any, is not shown and because many of the options shown above were sold in quantities in excess of 100 shares.

12

Chicago Board Options Exchange (CBOE)

Prior to April 1973, all option transactions took place in the over-the-counter market. However, in mid-1973, option trading began on a newly created exchange, the Chicago Board Options Exchange (CBOE). The accompanying reprint from *The Wall Street Journal* shows the transactions which took place on one day in 1974.

Chicago Board options basically resemble call options which have long been purchased and sold in the over-the-counter options market. However, they differ from non-Chicago-Board-call options in several respects, including: (1) the standardization of terms, (2) severance of the link between buyer and the writer by substitution of the Clearing Corporation as the primary obligor on every Chicago Board option, (3) the potential availability of a continuous secondary market for Chicago Board options, and (4) the absence of any adjustment of the exercise price of Chicago Board options due to the payment of cash

FIGURE 12-1

Chicago Board Options Exchange

Wednesday, June 5, 1974

Closing prices of all options. Sales unit is 100 shares. Security description includes exercise price.

	— Jul —		— Oct —		— Jan —		Stock
Option & price	Vol.	Last	Vol.	Last	Vol.	Last	Close
Am Tel 50	158	7-16	129	1¼	174	1 15-16	46¼
Atl R .. 90	280	4½	49	7⅛	3	9¾	91¾
Atl R .. 100	126	1⅜	42	3¾	b	b	91¾
Avon 90	a	a	b	b	b	b	....
Avon 80	a	a	b	b	b	b	....
Avon .. 70	225	⅛	b	b	b	b	51⅛
Avon 60	154	9-16	147	2⅛	b	b	51⅛
Avon .. 50	814	3⅛	128	5⅝	b	b	51⅛
Avon . 45	468	6⅜	34	8½	14	10¾	51⅛
Beth S . 30	206	1¾	93	2¾	25	3½	30⅛
Beth S 35	106	⅜	63	1 1-16	34	1¾	30⅛
Bruns . 20	77	¼	b	b	b	b	15½
Bruns . 15	187	1¼	156	2⅛	60	2¾	15½
Bruns 25	25	1-16	b	b	b	b	15½
Citicp 50	a	a	b	b	b	b	....
Citicp 45	15	¼	b	b	b	b	37⅜
Citicp . 40	78	1	30	2½	3	3¾	37⅜
Eas Kd 140	17	⅛	b	b	b	b	112
Eas Kd 120	286	1 11-16	62	5½	b	b	112
Eas Kd 100	319	13¼	45	16⅝	7	18¾	112
Exxon 100	3	⅛	b	b	b	b	75⅞
Exxon 90	116	¼	24	1 3-16	b	b	75⅞
Exxon . 80	208	1⅜	143	3¼	47	5½	75⅞
Exxon . 70	b	b	67	7¾	66	9¾	75⅞
Ford . 60	319	⅜	b	b	b	b	53¼
Ford 50	409	3¾	157	5⅛	74	6⅜	53¼
Ford .. 45	61	8⅛	21	9⅛	b	b	53¼
Ford 40	54	13	b	b	b	b	53¼
Glf Wn 25	282	1⅛	113	2¼	55	3⅛	24¼
Glf Wn 30	70	5-16	b	b	b	b	24¼
Gt Wst 20	462	1⅛	276	2	65	3	19
I B M 270	21	7-16	134	2⅞	b	b	220⅜
I B M 240	141	2¾	56	8⅝	15	12⅝	220⅜
I B M 220	b	b	68	17⅜	23	23	220⅜
I N A .. 35	9	¼	13	¾	b	b	28⅞
I N A .. 40	a	a	4	¼	b	b	28⅞
I N A .. 30	88	⅞	70	1⅞	50	2⅝	28⅞
I T T .. 35	a	a	b	b	b	b	....
I T T .. 30	18	⅛	82	9-16	b	b	21⅛
I T T .. 25	200	7-16	181	1 3-16	94	1 15-16	21⅛
I T T .. 20	249	2¼	98	3¼	97	4	21⅛
In Har .. 30	54	¼	45	13-16	b	b	25⅞
In Har . 35	a	a	b	b	b	b	.....
In Har 25	103	1 11-16	43	2½	22	3½	25⅞
Kerr M 65	10	⅝	a	a	2	9½	67¾
Kerr M 75	41	1½	18	3½	b	b	67¾
Kerr M 85	7	⅜	6	1⅝	b	b	67¾
Kresge 40	113	1	b	b	b	b	37⅜
Kresge 35	230	3⅜	46	4⅝	24	5⅝	37⅜
Kresge 30	46	7½	2	8¾	a	a	37⅜
Loews 25	8	1-16	7	⅜	b	b	16⅞
Loews 20	185	⅜	150	15-16	69	1½	16⅞
Loews 15	b	b	82	2⅝	88	3¼	16⅞
M M M 95	a	a	b	b	b	b	
M M M 85	22	⅜	b	b	b	b	75⅝
M M M 75	109	3	33	5½	8	7⅛	75⅝
Mc Don 60	236	2½	56	5⅛	b	b	56⅞
Mc Don 70	37	½	b	b	b	b	56⅞
Mc Don 50	82	8	7	10¾	[illegible]	11½	56⅞
Merck 90	53	1½	b	b	b	b	81¾
Merck 80	103	4¾	4	7⅜	[illegible]	8⅞	81¾
Monsan 70	247	2½	b	b	b	b	67⅝
Monsan 60	210	8⅝	66	10⅞	17	12¾	67⅝
Monsan 50	26	18	b	b	b	b	67⅝
Nw Air 25	597	2½	124	3½	70	4⅜	25⅞
Nw Air 20	131	6¼	33	7⅛	b	b	25⅞
Pnz U . 25	158	¼	36	½	57	1¼	19
Pnz U 250	78	5-16	9	1⅛	b	b	19
Pnz U .. 20	b	b	144	1⅝	104	2⅜	19
Polar .. 110	a	a	b	b	b	b	...
Polar .. 95	7	1-16	b	b	b	b	40
Polar .. 80	125	⅛	2	5-16	b	b	40
Polar .. 70	465	⅛	72	9-16	b	b	40
Polar .. 60	261	⅜	142	1¼	185	2¼	40
Polar .. 45	b	b	262	3⅞	116	5½	40
Polar .. 40	b	b	242	5½	59	8¼	40
R C A .. 25	3	⅛	b	b	b	b	16¾
R C A . 20	182	5-16	77	⅞	97	1¼	16¾
R C A .. 15	b	b	240	2⅝	b	b	16¾
R C A .. 65	b	b	b	b	92	3⅜	16¾
Sears .. 100	12	5-16	b	b	b	b	86¼
Sears .. 90	165	1⅜	24	3¾	b	b	86¼
Sears .. 80	41	7¼	4	9	1	10½	86¼
Sperry 40	222	1 15-16	25	3⅝	24	5	39⅞
Sperry . 45	83	½	46	1⅜	b	b	39⅞
Sperry .. 55	5	⅛	b	b	b	b	39⅞
Tex In 100	538	6⅜	77	11½	14	15⅛	100¼
Tex In 120	842	1⅜	132	4¾	b	b	100¼
Upjohn 85	580	4	b	b	b	b	84⅛
Upjohn 100	80	⅝	b	b	b	b	84⅛
Upjohn 65	181	19½	22	21¼	11	23¼	84⅛
Upjohn 75	b	b	24	13	8	17¼	84⅛
Weyerh 35	151	3¾	54	5¼	b	b	37⅝
Weyerh 40	224	1⅜	123	3	20	4⅛	37⅝
Weyerh 45	182	⅜	49	1¼	7	2¼	37⅝
Xerox 160	10	1-16	b	b	b	b	120
Xerox 140	38	⅝	b	b	b	b	120
Xerox 120	282	5¼	11	9⅞	12	12	120

Total volume 21,458. Open interest 304,097.
a—Not traded. b—Unavailable.

dividends to holders of the underlying stock. These four differences are discussed in detail below.

Standardization of Terms. Chicago Board options have standardized expiration dates and exercise prices, leaving the premium as the only variable, and this is determined in the Exchange marketplace.

Subject to certain limitations contained in the rules of the Exchange, a Chicago Board Option gives the holder the right commencing at the time it is issued and expiring at 10:30 A.M. on the last Monday of the expiration month (the "expiration date") to purchase from the Clearing Corporation the number of shares constituting the unit of trading of the underlying stock upon payment of the aggregate exercise price.*[1,2] Trading is generally opened in options having four fixed expiration months— January, April, July, and October. Trading in options of a particular expiration month commences approximately nine months earlier, so that at any given time there are open for trading options having at least three different expiration months. For example, in late January, shortly before January options expire, trading in options expiring in the following October will be opened (and trading in options expiring in April and July will previously have been opened.) At the time when trading is introduced in a new expiration month, the exercise price is fixed at a dollar-per-share figure most closely approximating the market price of the underlying stock. Exercise prices are fixed at 5-point intervals for stocks trading below 50; 10-point intervals for stocks trading between 50 and 100; and 20-point intervals for stocks trading above 100. Thus, if the market price of ABC stock is 53 when trading is initiated in October options, the exercise price would be set at 50.

When significant price movements take place in an underlying stock (during the quarterly periods between introductions of new expiration months in the manner described above), additional options with exercise prices reflecting such price movements may be opened for trading (at the price intervals stated above for one or more of the expiration months already the subject of trading). In the above example with respect to the opening of trading in ABC October 50s, if the market price of ABC stock were subsequently to decline to 45 trading in ABC October's might be introduced at that exercise price, and if the market price were then to rise to 60, ABC October's might also be introduced at that exercise price.

Once an option is opened for trading, trading in options having the same terms continues until 2:00 P.M. of the business day prior to the expiration date, unless trading is halted or suspended in accordance with Exchange rules.[3]

Severance of the Buyer-Writer Link. Whenever a Chicago Board option is issued to a holder there is a writer of an option having the same terms who is contractually obligated to the Clearing Corporation on account of that option. However, the holder of an option does not look to any particular writer for performance (or to a New York Stock Exchange firm); instead, the Clearing Corporation is the issuer of and obligor on every outstanding Chicago Board option, and its aggregate obligations to holders of options are backed up by the aggregate contractual obligations which writers owe to the Clearing Corporation. Upon exercise of an option, the Clearing Corporation assigns an exercise notice to a writer's clearing member selected at random, and the latter (who allocates the exercise notice to one or more of its customers if the option position is carried in a customer's account) is obligated to deliver the underlying stock against payment of the exercise price. In this respect Chicago Board options differ from options in the non-Chicago-Board-options market where each option has a buyer (holder) and a writer as well as an endorser who are contractually linked throughout the duration of the option, so that the original writer and endorser of a particular option are always obligated to the holder of that same option to deliver the underlying stock upon exercise.[4]

Secondary Market Prior to Option Expiration. The combination of standardization of terms and unlinking of specific holders and writers, as well as the provision of a central market for the purchase and sale of Chicago options, permits the existence of a continuous secondary market in which an existing position as holder or writer may be liquidated by an offsetting closing transaction. This secondary market enables a holder of a Chicago option to sell his option (in a "closing sale transaction") while it still has remaining life and to realize any market value it may then have. Similarly, such a secondary market permits the writer of a Chicago option to terminate his obligation by entering into a "closing purchase contract" on the exchange (which transaction has the effect of canceling his writer's obligation in consideration of the premium paid in such transaction).

Although the rules of the exchange are designed to provide a liquid secondary market in all options until the business day prior to their expiration (that is, all trading in an option ceases at the end of the business day prior to the expiration date of the option), there is no assurance that a liquid secondary market will exist for any particular option, and for some options no secondary market may exist. It is possible that a secondary market will not always exist for certain options either because of insufficient trading interest in those options or because the exchange has had to limit or suspend trading in those options. In either of these events, it might not be possible to effect closing transactions in particular options, with the result that a holder would have to exercise his option in order to realize any profit, and a writer would be unable to close out his position until the option expires or he is assigned an exercise notice. It should also be noted that a secondary market will not be beneficial to the holder of an option that has lost all of its value.

Closing Sale Example. A holder might have purchased an ABC July 50 option in January (when ABC stock was selling at 51) for an aggregate premium of $600 (plus a $25 commission). Three months later ABC stock is selling at 57 and ABC July 50 options are selling at 8½ (or $850 per option). In this situation, the holder would realize the $250 gain in the option price (less applicable commissions which in this example would aggregate $50) in a closing sale transaction. When the closing sale order is executed on the floor of the exchange, the holder's option position is extinguished and he can no longer exercise his option.

Just as the existence of a secondary market enables an option holder to liquidate his option position in the secondary market, so too does such a market permit a writer of an option to terminate his writer obligation by entering into a closing purchase transaction on the exchange. In such a transaction, the writer of an option "buys" an option having the same terms as the option he previously wrote. However, instead of the transaction's resulting in the issuance of an option, it has the effect of canceling the writer's pre-existing obligation.

Closing Purchase Transaction Example. A holder of 100 shares of ABC stock might have written an ABC July 50 option in January when ABC was selling at 51, and received an aggregate premium of $600 (less $25 commission). Three months later, ABC is selling at 47 and ABC July 50 options are at 2½, and the writer anticipates further decline in the price of the stock. Since his option has three months to run, selling his stock to eliminate any further loss would put him in the position of an uncovered writer (requiring that he maintain margin to cover his position) and would expose him to unlimited upside risk should the stock price rise. To avoid this risk, the writer might enter into a closing purchase transaction, paying $250 (plus an additional $25 commission) as the premium. This closes out his writer's position, leaving him free to sell ABC stock.

No Adjustment for Cash Dividends. Unlike options traded in the over-the-counter market, no adjustment is made to any of the terms of Chicago options to reflect the declaration or payment of ordinary cash dividends as defined in the rules of the exchange. However, if a writer is assigned an exercise notice by the Clearing Corporation prior to an ex-dividend date for a cash dividend, the exercising holder is entitled to that dividend. Both the number of shares underlying Chicago options and the exercise price are subject to adjustments in the event of dividends (other than ordinary cash dividends), distributions, stock splits, recapitalizations or reorganizations with respect to the underlying stock or the issuer thereof.

Adjustments to the terms of Chicago options are effective as of the "ex-date" of the event giving rise to the adjustment. Except as noted in the following paragraph, stock splits and other stock distributions which increase the number of outstanding shares of the issuer of the underlying stock have the effect of proportionately increasing the number of shares of underlying stock covered by the option and decreasing the exercise price. However, when a stock split or distribution results in the issuance of one or more whole shares for each outstanding share of underlying stock, the number of shares covered by the option is not adjusted. Instead the number of outstanding options is proportionately increased and the exercise price is proportionately decreased. This may be illustrated by comparing the adjustments to a single option covering 100 shares of stock at an exercise price of 60 resulting from a three-for-two stock distribution and a two-for-one stock distribution. In the former case, after adjustment, the option covers 150 shares at an exercise price of 40; while in the latter case, after adjustment there are two options covering 100 shares each at an exercise price of 30. In the case of other distributions (other than ordinary cash dividends), recapitalizations, or reorganizations by the issuer of the underlying stock, options with respect to such stock are equitably adjusted to cover the equivalent property or value which a holder of the underlying stock would be entitled to receive.

Margin Requirements. Regulation T of the Federal

Reserve Board and the rules of the Chicago Board Options Exchange, as well as the rules of other exchanges of which a broker may be a member, impose margin requirements with respect to a customer's positions as an option writer. Although, under exchange rules, brokers must require their customers to comply with either the exchange's margin rules or those of the New York Stock Exchange, these are minimum requirements, and many brokers impose more stringent requirements upon their option-writing customers. As a result of these requirements, all writing of transactions must be conducted in a margin account unless the writer owns the underlying stock and has agreed to deposit such stock promptly in a cash account with his broker. Brokers generally require writers to enter into margin agreements which give them a lien on the securities and other assets held in the margin account.

The following is a general summary of margin requirements applicable to writers under the rules of the Chicago Board Options Exchange.

1. The minimum margin that must be maintained on a daily basis in the margin account of an uncovered (naked) writer of an option is the greater of (a) 100 percent of the current market value of the option or (b) $250.* In addition, the option must be marked to the market on a daily basis—that is, *in addition* to the foregoing margin, the customer will have to maintain on deposit in the margin account an amount equal to 100 percent of the option's current market value (based upon its premium). (In determining the amount of margin required in an account, no value is ordinarily accorded to any option held in the account.)

2. As an exception to the requirement described in the first sentence of paragraph 1 above, in the event an uncovered (naked) writer holds in his account a security (including a Chicago Board option) exchangeable or con-

---

*From time to time, amounts substantially higher than $250 may be required, with the amount possibly depending upon the market price of the option.

vertible within 90 days without restriction other than the payment of money into the underlying stock, the minimum margin required to be maintained is 10 percent of the greater of the market value of such security or of the option. In addition, as described in the second sentence of paragraph 1, the option written must be marked to the market on a daily basis.

3. Margin is not required with respect to a covered writing position in an option. However, except as noted in paragraph 4 below, margin must be maintained with respect to the underlying stock position in the account in an amount equal to 25 percent of the current market price of the underlying stock or of the exercise price of the option, whichever is less.

4. A covered writer who has fully paid for the underlying stock may arrange for the "specific deposit" or "escrow deposit" of that stock. A specific deposit is an arrangement under which the writer's clearing member deposits the underlying stock with a depositary approved by the clearing corporation under an agreement which provides, among other things, that the deposited stock will be delivered at the order of the clearing corporation at any time while the clearing corporation holds a depositary receipt for the stock or upon the assignment of an exercise notice in respect of any option for which the deposit is made. An escrow deposit is an arrangement under which the customer arranges with a custodian holding the customer's stock to issue an escrow receipt to the Clearing Corporation, which provides for substantially the same delivery terms as described above for a specific deposit. *If the underlying stock is deposited under a specific deposit or escrow deposit, then no margin is required in respect of the option.*

The New York Stock Exchange's rules require an uncovered writing transaction to be margined as if the option had been exercised. This means, under its current rules, that 30 percent of the market value of the underlying stock must be maintained as equity in the margin account. In addition, the broker may also require the marking to the market of the underlying stock. New York Stock Exchange requirements for covered writing transactions are similar to the Chicago Exchange requirements set forth in paragraph 3 above. This description is not meant to be a complete statement of applicable margin requirements. Such requirements are very complex, and before engaging in a writing transaction the writer should determine from his broker the margin obligations that will be imposed.

Taxes

Tax Consequences to Holders of Options. The cost of an option is a nondeductible capital expenditure, and the option represents a capital asset in the hands of the holder. Gain or loss occurring upon the sale of an option in a closing sale transaction constitutes capital gain or loss, long-term or short-term depending upon how long the option has been held. If an option is allowed to expire, it is treated as having been sold on the expiration date.* Upon the exercise of an option, its cost is added to the exercise price to determine the basis of the underlying stock acquired.

Tax Consequences to Writers of Options. The premium received for writing an option is not included in income at the time of receipt (when the option is written), but is deferred until such time as the writer's obligation terminates. The writer's obligation may terminate (a) by passage of time, (b) by delivery of the underlying stock pursuant to the terms of the call, or (c) through a closing purchase transaction. If a writer's obligation terminates by reason of the passage of time, the premium constitutes ordinary income to the writer realized on the day of expiration.

*The resulting loss is a capital loss, and is short-term, depending on the holding period of the call.

If the option is exercised, the premium received by the writer is treated as an increase in the proceeds realized upon the sale of the underlying stock in the exercise transaction. The gain or loss on such sale constitutes capital gain or loss, long-term or short-term depending upon how long the stock has been held.

If a writer engages in a closing purchase transaction, thereby terminating his writer's obligation, the difference between the premium received in the original writing transaction and the amount paid in the closing transaction is *ordinary income or loss* realized on the day of the closing transaction.

Investors are advised to verify all tax questions with their own personal tax advisor, especially in light of the ever-changing opinions rendered by the judiciary.

Costs of Exchange Transactions

Exchange members charge commissions upon the purchase or writing of an option and upon the exercise of an option. The buyer of an option must pay a commission at the time of his opening purchase transaction, and must also pay a commission if he should elect to liquidate his position in a closing sale transaction or if he should exercise the option. Writers similarly are charged a commission on the opening sale transaction and also if they either engage in a closing purchase transaction or are required to deliver the underlying stock upon exercise. Commissions are based upon the dollars involved in a transaction, measured by the amount of the premium in the case of a purchase or sale transaction and by the aggregate exercise price of the underlying stock in the case of an exercise. In addition, writers in opening and closing sale transactions and exercise transactions may be charged the exchange's registration fee under the Securities Exchange Act of 1934, which is currently .05 percent of the premium.

The following tables set forth the minimum commissions chargeable by members to their nonmember customers (a) on the purchase or writing of an option and (b) on the exercise of an option with respect to that portion of an order involving not more than $30,000. (On that portion of an order involving an amount over $30,000, and with respect to orders aggregating under $100, the commission shall be as agreed between the customer and his broker.)

Orders for the Purchase, Sale, or Exercise of a Single Option

Premium Involved in the Order	*Minimum Commission*
$100–$2,499	1.3% + $12
$2,500–4,777	0.9% + 22
$4,778–29,999	65

Orders for the Purchase, Sale, or Exercise of Multiple Options

$100–2,499	1.3% + $12
$2,500–19,999	0.9% + 22
$20,000–29,999	0.6% + 82

Plus: First to tenth option covered by the order—$6 per option
Eleventh option and over covered by the order—$4 per option

Notwithstanding the foregoing, the minimum commissions on a single option order involving over $100 and under $30,000 shall be *not less than $25* nor more than $65, and the minimum commission per single option within a multiple option order shall not be more than the commission applicable to that option if it were in a single option order.

The following example illustrates the minimum commission charges imposed by exchange members upon their nonmember customers. In a transaction in which an option covering 100 shares of ABC stock at an exercise price of $100 per share is purchased by X and written by Y at a premium of $1,200 (which X pays to Y), X and Y must *each* pay his respective broker a minimum commission of $27.60 (1.3 percent of $1,200 plus $12). Should either X or Y subsequently liquidate his position in a closing transaction, *another commission* will have to be paid by him based upon the dollar amount of the premium involved in the closing transaction.

Should X exercise the option, paying $10,000 for the 100 shares of ABC, both X and the writer to whom the exercise notice is assigned will be required to pay their respective brokers a minimum commission of $65 for the purchase and sale of shares.

The nonmember commissions discussed above are minimum commissions, and exchange members may in some cases charge their nonmember customers commissions which are higher than these minimums.

Comparison of CBOE Brokerage Costs with a Negotiated Over-the-Counter Transaction

The writer of an option may sell on the CBOE or in the over-the-counter market. It can be assumed that the option buyer in either case will be willing to pay the same price for the option, including commissions. The writer will, of course, fare best by selling in the option market that leaves him the greatest sum after all costs—other things being equal.

Let us assume that stock ABC is selling at $20 per share, and that a call option on 100 shares is sold expiring six months later, and the premium paid by the *buyer* is $400. A comparison follows of the benefit to the option writer on the basis of two types of executions of the transaction—(a) over the counter and (b) on the CBOE.

	O-T-C	CBOE
Buyer pays $400*	.$400	$400
Writer's broker's endorsing fee	($6.25 to $12.50)	nil
Buyer's broker's endorsing fee	($6.25 to $12.50)	nil
Put and call dealer's spread	($12.50 or more)	nil
Buyer's brokerage commission	nil	($25)
Seller's brokerage commission	nil	($25)
Net to Seller of Option	$375 to $362.50	$350

*Actually the buyer pays $400 + $25 (minimum) commission. The seller receives $400 less $25 (minimum) commission. The difference between the buyer's cost, $425, and the sum the seller receives is $50.

Comparison of Minimum Margin Requirements of the Chicago Exchange to the New York Stock Exchange

When the stock involved in an option (call) sale is "long" in the writer's margin account and has been paid for in full neither the CBOE nor the NYSE impose any additional margin requirements. However when the stock in the account has not been paid for in full, the CBOE and the NYSE margin requirements differ. The following two cases should serve to illustrate those differences and the reader may refer back to the descriptions of margin requirements in previous sections to clarify the underlying rules.

Case 1. Sell 1 call on XYZ exercisable at $50. The stock price is currently $50 ($5,000 market value for 100 shares) and the option exercise price is also $5,000 for 100 shares.

CBOE	NYSE
The account equity (margin requirement) is the following: 25 percent of the lesser of (a) $5,000 (the current market price of the underlying stock) or (b) $5,000 (the option exercise price); i.e., $1,250 margin requirement.	The account equity must be maintained at 25 percent of the market price of the stock; i.e., $1,250 margin requirement.

Case II. Sell 1 call on XYZ exercisable at $50. The stock price is currently $90.

CBOE	NYSE
Equity must be 25 percent of the lesser of (a) $9,000 (market price of the stock), or (b) $5,000 (option exercise price); i.e., $1,250 margin requirement.	Equity must be 25 percent of the option price of the stock ($5,000); i.e., $1,250.

The writer of a naked call where the stock is not deposited in his margin account or covered by a depositary agreement, faces different margin requirements than those described above. These requirements are illustrated by the following three examples with respect to both CBOE and NYSE margin requirements.

The writer sells a naked call exercisable at $50 per share and the underlying stock is now selling at (1) $50 (and the option itself sells for $1,000); (2) at $60 and the option sells for $2,000; and (3) at $40 and the option sells for $200. The margin requirements are:

CBOE	NYSE
1. The requirement is the greater of 100% of the current market value of the option ($1,000) or $250; plus $1,000, the current market value of the option; i.e., total, $2,000 equity.	1. The requirement is 30% of the market value of the underlying stock, $5,000; i.e., $1,500, plus mark to market of the difference between the market price of the stock less the option striking price, or 0. Equity required, $1,500.
2. The greater of 100% of the current market value of the option, $2,000, or $250; plus $2,000, requirement total— $4,000.	2. 30% of market value of the stock, $6,000, is $1,800; mark-to-market is increase of $1,000; requirement is $2,800.
3. The greater of 100% of current market value of the option, $200, or $250; plus $200, i.e., total $450 requirement.	3. 30% of the market value of stock, $4,000, is $1,200; mark-to-market, decrease of $1,000; requirement is $200.

Summary: The CBOE offers both advantages and disadvantages to option investors, as have been described herein. A key additional advantage of the establishment of the CBOE has been to familiarize, through extensive publicity, many more potential investors with the role that options may play in helping such investors achieve their investment objectives.

FOOTNOTES TO CHAPTER 12

1. Chicago options are exercisable at any time after issuance until expiration, except as follows: (a) The exchange has provided limits on the number of options covering a given underlying stock which may be exercised* by a holder or group of holders acting in concert within any five consecutive business days. Unless otherwise determined and announced by the exchange, this limit is 1,000 option contracts† (which in most cases would cover 100,000 shares of the underlying stock). (b) the Board of Directors of the exchange is empowered to restrict, wholly or partially, the exercisability of options covering any one or more underlying securities if in its judgment such action is necessary for the maintenance of a fair and orderly market in the underlying stock or stocks. For the duration and to the extent of any such restriction, the holder of any such option will be unable to exercise it. However, commencing ten business days prior to an option's expiration date, no such restriction will remain in effect; instead the Board may impose a restriction on delivery of underlying stock not already owned by a writer to whom an exercise notice is assigned and may fix a daily settlement value for such option. In such case, in lieu of delivery and receipt of the underlying stock upon exercise, any such writer will be obligated to pay the settlement value fixed for the day the exercise notice is assigned, and any holder whose exercise notice is assigned to any such writer will not receive the underlying stock, but will be limited to receipt of such settlement value.

---

*The limits also apply to option writers.
†The 1,000 contract limit applies to options of a single class. A 500 contract limit applies to options of the same class and expiration date.

2. Chicago options may be purchased by placing an order with a broker, as for other types of securities. Orders should specify the underlying stock, expiration date and exercise price, the number of contracts to be purchased, and whether the purchase is an "opening" or "closing" transaction (the former being intended to result in a new position as a holder and the latter to close out a preexisting writer's position). In addition to the types of orders found generally in securities markets (that is market orders, limit orders, contingency orders, etc.), "spread orders," involving the purchase of one option and the concurrent sale of another option involving the same underlying stock but with different terms, are also available in the exchange's market. When a broker receives an order it is transmitted to the floor of the exchange for execution. If the broker for the buyer reaches agreement on the floor with a writer or his broker as to the premium, then a trade binding on both parties (but not yet on the Clearing Corporation) takes place. The brokers for both parties to the trade are each required to file a report of the trade with the Clearing Corporation, and the broker for the buyer is required (through a Clearing member) to pay the premium to the Clearing Corporation prior to 9:00 A.M. of the following business day. If the reports of the two parties are in agreement and if the premium has been paid, the option is issued by the Clearing Corporation at 10:00 A.M. on the business day following the trade. In the event the reports do not match, the option will be issued at 10:00 A.M. on the first business day following the day on which the Clearing Corporation receives a report that the differences have been reconciled.

3. Trading halts in both opening and closing transactions in one or more options may be imposed by exchange floor officials for up to two consecutive business days whenever such action is considered advisable in the interests of a fair and orderly market, taking into consideration such factors as trading suspensions or other trading irregularities with respect to any underlying stock, or other unusual circumstances. Trading suspensions for longer periods may be imposed by the Exchange's board on the basis of similar factors.

4. Outstanding Chicago options may be exercised at any time prior to 10:30 A.M. on the last Monday of the specified expiration month by the tender of an exercise notice to the Clearing Corporation. An exercise notice may be so tendered only by the Clearing member in whose account the option is held with the Clearing Corporation and only in a form acceptable to the Clearing Corporation. This means that a holder of an option may only exercise it through the broker handling the account in which the option is held. In order for clearing members to be able to meet the expiration deadline referred to above, exchange members have established earlier time limits for their customers to instruct them to exercise an option. Each customer should determine from his broker the time limit so established, since a customer's failure to instruct his broker to exercise an option prior to this time will mean that the option cannot be exercised. It should be noted that trading in an option ceases one business day prior to its expiration date. After that time closing writing transactions will not be possible and a holder will be able to realize any profit in an option only through the timely submission of an exercise notice. If an exercise notice is properly tendered to the Clearing Corporation prior to 12:00 noon on any business day prior to the expiration date, or prior to 10:30 A.M. on the expiration date, the Clearing Corporation will assign the exercise notice on that business day. An exercise notice tendered after 12:00 noon on any day prior to the expiration date will be assigned on the following business day. The exercise notice will be assigned to a randomly selected Clearing member (by computer) which has an account with the Clearing Corporation reflecting the writing of an option or options having the same terms as the exercised option. In its random selection procedures the Clearing Corporation may classify the writer positions of Clearing members by type of account, by size of transaction (so that exercise notices in respect of 25 or more options having the same terms will be assigned to a writer of 25 or more such options), and by type of margin deposited with the Clearing Corporation. If the Clearing Corporation assigns an exercise notice to a member's account, the member will allocate the exercise notice to a customer maintaining a position as a writer in the account. This allocation by the member may be upon a random selection basis, a "first in, first out" basis, or any other method

chosen by the member that is fair and equitable to its customers. Members must report their chosen method of allocation to the exchange, and may not change a method of allocation unless the change is also reported to the exchange. Customers may request that their brokers inform them of the method used in assigning exercise notices to the accounts of writers. The latest assignments of exercise notices to Clearing members are made at approximately 9:00 P.M. on the expiration date. Each writer should determine from his broker the latest time prior to which the broker may notify the writer that an exercise notice has been assigned to him. The Clearing member to whom an exercise notice is assigned is required to deliver the underlying stock in good deliverable form on or before 12:00 noon on the "exercise settlement date" against payment of the aggregate exercise price. The exercise settlement date is the fifth business day following the date on which the exercise notice is assigned with certain exceptions. The exercising Clearing member must accept delivery and make the required payment if the underlying stock is delivered in a unit of trading (generally 100 shares) or any multiple thereof. Upon delivery of the underlying stock to the Clearing member representing the exercising holder, the obligations of the Clearing Corporation will be completely discharged and the Clearing Corporation will have no responsibility if the Clearing member should fail to deliver the underlying stock to or upon the order of the exercising holder.

5. An option that is bought or sold on the CBOE can only be liquidated on the CBOE. Likewise, an option which is bought or sold off the CBOE (in the over-the-counter market) cannot be liquidated on the CBOE.

13

An Option Account
in Operation

The author has managed only one account on a purely discretionary basis from the inception of the account. This account must be described as aggressive because above average calculated risks are taken in order to seek a high annual rate of return.

A summary follows of the results of the account from its inception on February 28, 1973, through Friday, June 29, 1973.

Market value of securities long ($41,990) after deduction of loss, where applicable, today, if naked options sold were exercised ($4,116)	$37,574
Plus: Cash balance with brokers	9,229
Less: Interest, if any, on amounts owed to brokers for the period from June 29, 1973, until the date of expiry of the last option to expire	0
Less: Estimated brokerage cost to sell securities long in the account.............................	(630)
Less: Estimated brokerage cost to buy and sell securities under naked options where the present market price is adverse compared to the option striking price	(1,004)
Net equity at June 29, 1973, closing prices	$45,169
Less: Cash employed (cash outlay)	32,053
Estimated net profit at June 29, 1973.............	$13,116

Return on Investment

$$\frac{\text{Net profit} - \$13,116}{\text{Cash employed} - \$32,053} = 41\%$$

for a period of investment of four months. The date on which the last currently written option expires is January 7, 1974. From the inception of the account on February 28, 1973, to January 7, 1974, is a period of about 10 months. The estimated annualized rate of return based on the present situation is then:

$$\frac{12 \text{ months}}{10 \text{ months}} \times 41\% = 49\% \text{ annualized}$$

No allowance is included above for accrued dividends or for federal, state, or local income or ad valorem taxes.

The net profit above is of course contingent, and a final profit figure will only be known if the account becomes dormant and all existing option positions are eliminated either by exercise, expiration, or offsetting transactions.

The position at June 29 may improve or it may worsen— even if no further transactions in the form of new positions are taken. This could occur as follows: improvement would take place if appreciation takes place in the market value of securities long in the account, where such securities are at present below their respective option-striking prices; improvement would also take place if there is a decline in the market value of securities on which naked call options have been sold which are priced at present above the option striking price; improvement would also result from an increase in the market price on securities on which naked put options have been sold in instances in which the present market price is below the put option striking price. Deterioration of the present position would occur in the reverse situations.

For those readers interested in pursuing further the details of the transactions that gave the above results, the following pages set forth the consolidated figures (several brokerage accounts combined together).

From a traditional accounting viewpoint, in the financial statements below, there are two significant changes from the presentation set forth above, as follows: (1) Investments in securities long are shown at cost. (2) Option premiums are carried as a liability item even though the cash with respect thereto has been received, until the particular options are either exercised or expire. At June 29, 1973, no options had either been exercised or expired.

Balance Sheet
June 29, 1973

Assets:

Cash	$ 9,229
Investments in securities (at cost; market value–$41,990).........................	51,044
Total assets	$60,273

Liabilities:

Premiums received from options sold, but not yet expired, offset, or exercised	$28,231

Capital:

Investor's cash outlay	32,053
Retained earnings.........................	(11)
Total liabilities and capital	$60,273

Statement of Income for the Four-Month Period
March 1, 1973 through June 29, 1973

Dividends	$14
Less: Interest expense	25
Net loss	$11

FIGURE 13-1

Page 1 NAME OF ACCOUNT: Lawrence R. Rosen   A/C NO:_____   TYPE A/C: [x] General Margin [ ] Conv. Bond [ ] Muni. Bond [ ] Other

BROKERAGE FIRM:_____   BROKER'S NAME:_____   BROKER'S PHONE:_____

Date	Stk.	Quantity	Price S.P.	Price Prem.	Invest. Cost	Deferred Premium Income	Option Expiry	Divid. Income	Interest Charges	Sales Proceeds	Gain/Loss Long Term	Short Term	Other	Cash Outlays	Dr.	Cr.	Bal.
2-28-73	Mattel	400		6	2,467.20		9-10-73								2,467.20		(2,467.20)
2-28-73	Mattel	4 calls	6	1 3/8		550.00										550.00	(1,917.20)
3-1-73	Cash deposit													1,917.20		1,917.20	-0-
3-23-73	Merrill-Lynch	100		17 7/8	1,822.74		10-03-73								1,822.74		(1,822.74)
3-23-73	MER	1 call	17 7/8	2 1/2		250.00										250.00	(1,572.74)
3-30-73	Levitz	100		13 1/2	1,379.55										1,379.55		(2,952.29)
3-30-73	Levitz	1 call	13 1/2	2 1/2		250.00	10-10-73									250.00	(2,702.29)
3-30-73	Cash deposit													647.00		647.00	(2,055.29)
3-8 & 3-21	Interest @ 9% & 9¼%								2.45						2.45		(2,057.74)
									6.81						6.81		(2,064.55)
4-17-73	Interest @ 7½								1.72						1.72		(2,066.27)
4-13-73	Coastal States Gas	200		17 1/8	3,464.60										3,464.60		(5,530.87)
4-17-73	Coastal	2 calls	17 3/4	2 3/4		550.00	10-22-73									550.00	(4,980.87)
4-17-73	U.S. Homes	300		11 1/2	3,521.05										3,521.05		(8,501.92)
4-17-73	U.S. Homes	3 calls	11 1/2	2 1/8		637.50	10-29-73									637.50	(7,864.42)
4-18-73	Levitz	1 call	10 3/4	1 5/16		131.25	7-23-73									131.25	(7,733.17)
4-19-73	UH	3 calls	9 7/8	2 1/8		637.50	10-29-73									637.50	(7,095.67)
4-19-73	Hardees	200		12	2,455.20										2,455.20		(9,550.87)
4-19-73	H	2 calls	12	2 1/8		425.00	10-29-73									425.00	(9,125.87)
4-19-73	Merrill	1 call	16	2 1/4		225.00	10-29-73									225.00	(8,900.87)
4-24-73	Cash deposit													5,826.00		5,826.00	(3,074.87)
4-24-73	Magnavox	200		14 1/4	2,909.65										2,909.65		(5,984.52)
4-24-73	MAG	2 calls	14 1/4	2 1/2		500.00	11-5-73									500.00	(5,484.52)
4-27-73	Deltona	100		13 1/2	1,379.55										1,379.55		(6,864.07)
4-27-73	DLT	1 put	13 5/8			400.00	11-06-73									400.00	(6,464.07)
4-27-73	DLT	1 call	13 5/8				11-06-73										
5-14-73	Levitz	1 call	7 3/4	1 7/8		187.50	11-26-73									187.50	(6,276.57)
5-14-73	Deposit													1,857.00		1,857.00	(4,419.57)
5-17-73	Driver-Harris	2 calls	9	1 3/4		350.00	11-27-73									350.00	(4,069.57)
5-18-73	Jewel Cor	4 calls	11 1/8	2 1/4		900.00	11-28-73									900.00	(3,169.57)
	Subtotals				19,399.54	5,993.75			10.98					10,247.20			

FIGURE 13-1 (Continued)

Page 2 NAME OF ACCOUNT: Lawrence R. Rosen   A/C NO: _____   TYPE A/C: [x] General Margin / [ ] Conv. Bond / [ ] Muni Bond / [ ] Other

BROKERAGE FIRM: _____   BROKER'S NAME: _____   BROKER'S PHONE: _____

Date	Stk.	Quantity	Price S.P.	Price Prem.	Invest. Cost	Deferred Premium Income	Option Expiry	Divid. Income	Interest Charges	Sales Proceeds	Gain or Loss Long Term	Short Term	Other	Cash Outlays	Brokerage A/C Balance Dr.	Cr.	Bal.
5-18-73	Balance Bgt. Forward				19,399.54	5,993.75								10,247.20			(3,169.57)
5-24-73	First Sav. & Loan	500	12 7/8		6,547.44				10.98						6,547.44		(9,717.01)
5-24-73	FSX	5 calls	12 7/8	2 7/16		1,218.75	12-4-73									1,218.75	(8,498.26)
5-73	Interest 7 1/2-7 3/4%								14.53						14.53		(8,512.79)
5-73	Merrill Ly. Dividend							14.00								14.00	(8,498.79)
5-30-73	Cash deposit													3,006.00		3,006.00	(5,492.79)
5-23-73	Univ. Sav. Assn.	5 calls	8	1 9/16		781.25	12-3-73									781.25	(4,711.54)
5-21-73	USV	500			4,024.94										4,024.94		(8,736.48)
5-21-73	MAG	2 calls	11 3/8	7 7/8		375.00	12-3-73									375.00	(8,361.48)
5-21-73	Levitz	1 call	6 3/8	1 1/4		125.00	12-3-73									125.00	(8,236.48)
5-21-73	Combustion Equip.	5 calls	14 3/4	2 7/8		1,437.50	12-3-73									1,437.50	(6,798.98)
5-21-73	Faberge	200 @	7 7/8		1,588.53										1,588.53		(8,387.51)
5-21-73	FBG	300 @	8		2,474.25										2,474.25		(10,861.76)
5-21-73	FBG	3 calls	9 7/8	1 1/2		750.00	12-3-73									750.00	(10,111.76)
5-21-73	Lennar	500	9		4,592.50										4,592.50		(14,704.26)
5-21-73	LEN	5 calls	9	1 7/8		937.50	12-3-73									937.50	(13,766.76)
5-21-73	Litton	2 calls	7 3/8	1 3/8		275.00	11-28-73									275.00	(13,491.76)
5-21-73	LIT	5 calls	6 7/8	1 3/8		687.50	12-3-73									687.50	(12,804.26)
5-21-73	Skyline	2 calls	14	2 3/4		550.00	12-3-73									550.00	(12,254.26)
5-21-73	TWA w/s	400	9 7/8		4,031.55										4,031.55		(16,285.81)
5-21-73	TWA w/s	4 calls	9 7/8	1 1/2		600.00	8-24-73									600.00	(15,685.81)
5-25-73	Cash deposit													10,400.00		10,400.00	(5,285.81)
5-30-73	MER	1 call	14 3/8	2 1/8		212.50	12-10-73									212.50	(5,073.31)
5-29-73	Filter Dynamics	3 calls	9 1/2	2		600.00	12-10-73									600.00	(4,473.31)
	Open Road	3 calls	12 1/2	2 1/2		750.00	12-10-73									750.00	(3,723.31)
	Coastal States Gas	1 call	11 5/8	2		200.00	12-10-73									200.00	(3,523.31)
	CGP	1 call	11 1/2	1 3/8		137.50	9-4-73									137.50	(3,385.81)
	Extendicare	100	7 7/8		809.65										809.65		(4,195.46)
	XTC	1 call	7 7/8	1 7/8		187.50	12-10-73									187.50	(4,007.96)
	Subtotals				43,468.40	15,818.75		14.00	25.51					23,653.20			

FIGURE 13-1 (Continued)

Page 3

NAME OF ACCOUNT: Lawrence R. Rosen A/C NO: _____

TYPE A/C: [X] General Margin [ ] Conv. Bond [ ] Muni. Bond [ ] Other

BROKERAGE FIRM: _____ BROKER'S NAME: _____ BROKER'S PHONE: _____

Date	Stk.	Quantity	Price S.P.	Price Prem.	Invest. Cost	Deferred Premium Income	Option Expiry	Divid. Income	Interest Charges	Sales Proceeds	Gain/Loss Long Term	Gain/Loss Short Term	Gain/Loss Other	Cash Outlays	Brokerage A/C Dr.	Brokerage A/C Cr.	Brokerage A/C Bal.
5-73	Balance Bgt Fwd				43,468.40	15,818.75		14.00	25.51					23,653.20			(4,007.96)
	Peter Paul Ind.	200	18 3/8	18 3/8	3,742.08		8-2-73								3,742.08		(7,750.04)
	PPI	2 calls	15 7/8	1 7/8		375.00	8-2-73									375.00	(7,375.04)
5-30-73	Frigitronics	2 calls	7	2		400.00	8-2-73									400.00	(6,975.04)
5-31-73	Winnebago	2 calls	6 5/8	1 3/4		350.00	12-10-73									350.00	(6,625.04)
5-30-73	Winnebago	3 calls	10 1/8	1 3/4		525.00	12-10-73									525.00	(6,100.04)
6-1-73	Sierra Pac. Ind.	3 calls	9 7/8	1 3/8		412.50	9-4-73									412.50	(5,687.54)
6-4-73	Coastal States Gas	2 calls		1 7/8		375.00	12-11-73									375.00	(5,312.54)
	Amer. Medicorp	200	4 1/4		879.80		12-14-73										(6,192.34)
	AAM	2 calls	8	1		200.00	12-14-73									200.00	(5,992.34)
	STP	1 call		1 3/4		175.00	12-17-73									175.00	(5,817.34)
6-5-73	Deposit – cash													7,000.00		7,000.00	1,182.66
6-7-73	Wheelabrator	1 call	10 5/8	2 1/8		212.50	12-18-73									212.50	1,395.16
6-8-73	Brad Regan	2 calls	8 5/8	1 7/8		375.00	12-18-73									375.00	1,770.16
	Leadership Hous.	2 calls	4 7/8	1 1/16		212.50	9-11-73									212.50	1,982.66
6-11-73	Pier 1	3 calls	7 3/4	1 1/8		337.50	12-21-73									337.50	2,320.16
6-12-73	Brad Regan	1 call	8 1/8	1 7/8		187.50	12-24-73									187.50	2,507.66
6-8-73	Memorex	1 call	5 1/4	1		100.00	9-11-73									100.00	2,607.66
6-14-73	Atlas Consol. Mine	2 calls	18 5/8	2 3/8		475.00	12-24-73									475.00	3,082.66
6-14-73	Deposit – Cash													700.00		700.00	3,782.66
6-1-73	Pall	2 calls	11	2 1/8		425.00	12-11-73									425.00	4,207.66
6-4-73	Levitz	2 calls	6 7/8	1 3/8		275.00	12-11-73									275.00	4,482.66
6-4-73	Merrill Ly.	1 call	13 5/8	2		200.00	12-11-73									200.00	4,682.66
6-4-73	Bowmar	1 call	22	5 1/4		525.00	9-10-73									525.00	5,207.66
6-7-73	Buttes	1 call	31 3/8	2 3/8		237.50	9-14-73									237.50	5,445.16
6-11-73	ITT	1 call		3 1/4		325.00										325.00	5,770.16
6-12-73	Eastern Air.	300	9 3/4		2,953.49										2,953.49		2,816.67
6-12-73	EAL	3 calls	17 1/2	1 3/4		525.00	12-21-73									525.00	3,341.67
6-14-73	Frigitronics	1 call		2 1/4		225.00	9-19-73									225.00	3,566.67
	Subtotals				51,043.77	23,268.75		14.00	25.51						31,353.20			

FIGURE 13-1 (Concluded)

Page 4 NAME OF ACCOUNT: Lawrence R. Rosen A/C NO: _____

BROKERAGE FIRM: _____ BROKER'S NAME: _____ BROKER'S PHONE: _____

TYPE A/C: [X] General Margin [ ] Conv. Bond [ ] Muni. Bond [ ] Other

Date	Stk.	Quantity	Price S.P.	Prem.	Invest. Cost	Deferred Premium Income	Option Expiry	Divid. Income	Interest Charges	Sales Proceeds	Gain or Loss Long Term	Short Term	Other	Cash Outlays	Dr.	Cr.	Bal.
6-15-73	Bal. Bgt. Fwd.				51,043.77	23,268.75		14.00	25.51					31,353.20			+3,566.67
6-15-73	Duplan	2 calls	6 3/4	1 3/8		275.00	12-26-73									275.00	+3,841.67
6-15-73	Amer. Tr. Serv.	2 calls	11 1/4	2 1/4		450.00	12-26-73									450.00	+4,291.67
6-15-73	Memorex	1 call	4 7/8	1		100.00	12-26-73									100.00	+4,391.67
6-15-73	Jewel Cor	2 calls	9 5/8	2 1/8		425.00	12-26-73									425.00	+4,816.67
6-18-73	Amer. Tr. Serv.	3 calls	11 3/8	2 1/2		750.00	12-28-73									750.00	+5,566.67
6-19-73	Mattel	2 calls	5 1/8	1		200.00	12-28-73									200.00	+5,766.67
6-19-73	Rockower	1 call	9 1/4	7/8		187.50	12-31-73									187.50	+5,954.17
6-21-73	TWA W/S	4 calls	7 1/4	3/4		700.00	11-30-73									700.00	+6,654.17
6-21-73	TWA W/S	3 calls	4 7/8	1 1/2		450.00	11-30-73									450.00	+7,104.17
6-22-73	MAG	1 call	10 1/4	1 7/8		187.50	12-31-73									187.50	+7,291.67
6-22-73	Winnebago	1 call	5 3/8	1 1/4		125.00	1-2-74									125.00	+7,416.67
6-25-73	Telex	5 calls	3 7/8	(1)		500.00	1-4-74									500.00	+7,916.67
6-27-73	Memorex	1 call	5 1/8	1 1/8		112.50	1-7-74									112.50	+8,029.17
6-27-73	Telex	5 calls	3 7/8	(1)		500.00	1-7-74									500.00	+8,529.17
6-28-73	Cash deposit													700.00		700.00	+9,229.17
	Totals				51,043.77	28,231.25		14.00	25.51					32,053.20			

FIGURE 13-2

Page 1 of 4

PORTFOLIO EVALUATION AT 6-29-73

Date	Stock	Quantity	Price S.P.	Price Prem.	Invest. Cost	Deferred Premium Income	Option Expiry	6-29-73 Closing Market Prices	Securities Long Market Value	All Options— Hedged and Naked Exposure	Market Value of Naked Options in Adverse Position
2-28-73	Mattel	400		6	2,467.20			4 1/2	1,800.00		
2-28-73	Mattel	4 calls	6	1 3/8		550.00	9-10-73	4 1/2			
3-1-73	Cash Deposit										
3-23-73	Merrill Lynch	100		17 7/8	1,822.74			13 1/8	1,313.00		
3-23-73	MER	1 call	17 7/8	2 1/2		250.00	10-03-73	13 1/8			
3-30-73	Levitz	100		13 1/2	1,379.55			6	600.00		
3-30-73	Levitz	1 call	13 1/2	2 1/2		250.00	10-10-73	6			
3-30-73	Cash Deposit										
3-8 & 3/21	Interest @ 9% & 9 1/4%										
4-17-73	Interest @ 7 1/2%										
4-13-73	Coastal States Gas	200		17 1/8	3,464.60			7 1/4*	1,425.00		
4-17-73	Coastal	2 calls	17 3/4	2 3/4		550.00	10-22-73	7 1/4*			
4-17-73	U.S. Homes	300		11 1/2	3,521.05			8 1/2	2,550.00		
4-17-73	U.S. Homes	3 calls	11 1/2	2 5/8		637.50	10-29-73	8 1/2			
4-18-73	Levitz	1 call	10 3/4	1 5/16		131.25	7-23-73	6			
4-19-73	UH	3 calls	9 7/8	2/8		637.50	10-29-73	8 1/2			
4-19-73	Hardees	200		12	2,455.20			13	2,600.00		
4-19-73	H	2 calls	12	2 1/8		425.00	10-29-73	13			
4-23-73	Merrill	1 call	16	2 1/4		225.00	10-29-73	13 1/8		200.00	
4-24-73	Cash Deposit										
4-24-73	Magnavox	200		14 1/4	2,909.65			8 3/4	1,750.00		
4-24-73	MAG	2 calls	14 1/4	2 1/2		500.00	11-5-73	8 3/4			
4-27-73	Deltona	100		13 1/2	1,379.55			11	1,100.00		
4-27-73	DLT	1 put	7 3/4	13 5/8		400.00	11-06-73	11			
4-27-73	DLT	1 call		13 5/8		187.50	11-06-73	11			
5-14-73	Levitz	1 call		17 7/8			11-26-73	6	263.00		
5-14-73	Deposit										
5-17-73	Driver-Harris	2 calls	9	1 3/4		350.00	11-27-73	9 3/4		150.00	
5-18-73	Jewel Cor	4 calls	2 1/4	11 1/8		900.00	11-28-73	8 3/4			

* Trading suspended
7 1/4 close prior thereto

FIGURE 13-2 *(Continued)*

Page 2 of 4

Date	Stock	Quantity	Price S.P.	Price Prem.	Invest. Cost	Deferred Premium Income	Option Expiry	6-29-73 Closing Market Prices	Securities Long Market Value	All Options—Hedged and Naked Exposure	Market Value of Naked Options in Adverse Position
5-18-73	Balance Bgt. Fwd				19,399.54	5,993.75					
5-24-73	First Savings & Loan	500	12 7/8		6,547.44			12 1/8	6,063.00		
5-24-73	FSX	5 calls	12 7/8	2 7/16		1,218.75	12-4-73	12 1/8			
5-73	Interest 7 1/2 – 7 3/4%										
5-73	Merrill Ly. Dividend										
5-30-73	Cash Deposit										
5-23-73	Univ. Savings Assn.	5 calls	8	1 9/16	4,024.94	781.25	12-3-73	7 3/4			
5-21-73	USV	500						7 3/4	3,875.00		
5-21-73	MAG	2 calls	11 3/8	1 7/8		375.00	12-3-73	8 3/4			
5-21-73	Levitz	1 call	6 3/8	1 1/4		125.00	12-3-73	6			
5-21-73	Combustion Equip.	5 calls	14 3/4	2 7/8		1,437.50	12-3-73	15 1/2			7,750.00
5-21-73	Faberge 200 @ 7 7/8	200 @	7 7/8		1,588.53			9 1/8	4,563.00		
5-21-73	FBG 300 @ 8	300 @	8		2,474.25			9 1/8		375.00	
5-21-73	FBG	3 calls	7 7/8	1 1/2		750.00	12-3-73	9 1/8		338.00	
5-21-73	FBG	2 calls						9 1/8		250.00	
5-21-73	Lennar	500			4,592.50			8 7/8	4,438.00		
5-21-73	LEN	5 calls	9	1 7/8		937.50	12-3-73	8 7/8			
5-21-73	Litton	2 calls	7 3/8	1 3/8		275.00	11-28-73	8 3/8		200.00	
5-21-73	LIT	5 calls	6 7/8	1 3/8		687.50	12-3-73	8 3/8		750.00	5,863.00
5-21-73	Skyline	2 calls	14	2 3/4		550.00	12-3-73	16 1/8		425.00	3,225.00
5-21-73	TWA W/S	400			4,031.55			5 5/8	2,250.00		
5-21-73	TWA W/S	4 calls	9 7/8	1 1/2		600.00	8-24-73	5 5/8			
	Cash Deposit										
5-25-73	Merrill	1 call	14 3/8	2 7/8		212.50	12-10-73	13 1/8			
5-30-73	Filter Dynamics	3 calls	9 1/2	2		600.00	12-10-73	7 1/8			
5-29-73	Open Road	3 calls	12 1/2	2 1/2		750.00	12-10-73	10 1/2			
	Coastal States Gas	1 call	11 5/8	2		200.00	12-10-73	7 1/4*			
	CGP	1 call	11 1/2	1 3/8		137.50	9-4-73	7 1/4*			
	Extendicare	100	7 7/8		809.65			6 5/8	663.00		
	XTC	1 call	7 7/8	1 7/8		187.50	12-10-73	6 5/8			

FIGURE 13-2 *(Continued)*
Page 3 of 4

Date	Stock	Quantity	Price		Invest. Cost	Deferred Premium Income	Option Expiry	6-29-73 Closing Market Prices	Securities Long Market Value	All Options—Hedged and Naked Exposure	Market Value of Naked Options in Adverse Position
			S.P.	Prem.							
5-73	Balance Bgt. Fwd.	200		18 3/8	43,468.40	15,818.75		16 7/8	3,375.00		
	Peter Paul Ind.	2 calls	18 3/8	17 7/8	3,742.00	375.00	8-2-73	16 7/8			
	PPI	2 calls	15 7/8	2		400.00	8-2-73	13 3/8			
5-30-73	Frigitronics	2 calls	7	1 3/4		350.00	12-10-73	5			
5-31-73	Winnebago	3 calls	6 5/8	1 3/4		525.00	12-10-73	5			
5-30-73	Winnebago	3 calls	10 1/8	1 3/8		412.50	9-4-73	8 7/8			
6-1-73	Sierra Pac. Ind.	2 calls	9 7/8	1 7/8		375.00	12-11-73	7 1/4*			
6-4-73	Coastal States Gas	200		4 1/4	879.80			4 1/4	850.00		
	Amer. Medicorp.	2 calls	4 1/4	1		200.00	12-14-73	4 1/4			
	AAM	1 call	8	1 3/4		175.00	12-14-73	7 5/8			
	STP	1 call									
	Deposit-Cash										
6-5-73	Wheelabrator	1 call	10 5/8	2 1/8		212.50	12-17-73	11		38.00	1,100.00
6-7-73	Brad Regan	2 calls	8 5/8	1 7/8		375.00	12-18-73	8 1/4			
6-8-73	Leadership Hous.	2 calls	4 7/8	1 1/16		212.50	12-18-73	4 5/8			
6-11-73	Pier 1	3 calls	7 3/4	1 1/8		337.50	9-11-73	7 3/8			
6-12-73	Brad Regan	1 call	8 1/8	1 7/8		187.50	12-21-73	8 1/4		13.00	825.00
6-8-73	Memorex	1 call	5 1/4	1		100.00	12-24-73	5 1/4			
6-14-73	Atlas Consol. Mine	2 calls	18 5/8	2 3/8		475.00	9-11-73	23		875.00	4,600.00
6-14-73	Deposit-Cash										
	Pall	2 calls	11	2 1/8		425.00	12-24-73	11			
	Levitz	2 calls	6 7/8	1 3/8		275.00	12-11-73	6			
6-4-73	Merrill	1 call	13 5/8	2		200.00	12-11-73	13 1/8			
6-4-73	Bowmar	1 call	23 7/8	5 1/4		525.00	12-11-73	26		213.00	2,600.00
6-7-73	Buttes	1 call	22	2 3/8		237.50	9-10-73	24 1/2		250.00	2,450.00
6-11-73	ITT	1 call	31 3/8	3 1/4		325.00	9-14-73	30 3/8			
6-12-73	Eastern Air.	300		9 5/8	2,953.49			9 1/4	2,775.00		
6-12-73	EAL	3 call	9 3/4	1 3/4		525.00	12-21-73	9 1/4			
6-14-73	Frigitronics	1 call	17 1/2	2 1/4		225.00	9-19-73	13 3/8			

FIGURE 13-2 *(Concluded)*

Page 4 of 4

Date	Stock	Quantity	Price S.P.	Price Prem.	Invest. Cost	Deferred Premium Income	Option Expiry	6-29-73 Closing Market Prices	Securities Long Market Value	All Options—Hedged and Naked Exposure	Market Value of Naked Options in Adverse Position
6-15-73	Bal. Bgt. Fwd.				51,043.77	23,268.75					
6-15-73	Duplan	2 calls	6 3/4	1 3/8		275.00	12-26-73	5 7/8			
6-15-73	Amer. Tr. Serv.	2 calls	11 1/4	2 1/4		450.00	12-26-73	10 3/8			
6-15-73	Memorex	1 call	4 7/8	1		100.00	12-26-73	5 1/4		38.00	525.00
6-15-73	Jewel Cor	2 calls	9 5/8	2 1/8		425.00	12-26-73	8 3/4			
6-18-73	Amer. Tr. Serv.	3 calls	11 3/8	2 1/2		750.00	12-28-73	10 3/8			
6-18-73	Mattel	2 calls	5 1/8			200.00	12-28-73	4 1/2			
6-19-73	Rockower	1 call	9 1/4	1 7/8		187.50	12-31-73	9 1/2		25.00	950.00
6-19-73	TWA W/S	4 calls	7 1/4	1 3/4		700.00	11-30-73	5 5/8			
6-21-73	TWA W/S	3 calls	4 7/8	1 1/2		450.00	11-30-73	5 5/8			
6-22-73	MAG	1 call	10 1/4	1 7/8		187.50	12-31-73	8 3/4			
6-22-73	Winnebago	1 call	5 3/8	1 1/4		125.00	1-2-74	5			
6-25-73	Telex	5 calls	3 7/8	(1)		500.00	1-4-74	3 3/4			
6-27-73	Memorex	1 call	5 1/8	1 1/8		112.50	1-7-74	5 1/4		13.00	525.00
6-27-73	Telex	5 calls	3 7/8	(1)		500.00	1-7-74	3 3/4			
6-28-73	Cash Deposit										
	Totals				51,043.77	28,231.25			41,990.00	4,116.00	33,463.00

MARKET VALUE SECURITIES LONG $41,990.00

Less: ALL OPTIONS (HEDGED & NAKED) EXPOSURE 4,116.00

EQUITY – EXCLUSIVE OF CASH POSITION $37,874.00

BROKERAGE COST TO SELL SECURITIES LONG: $41,990 @ 1.5% = $630.00

BROKERAGE COST TO BUY & SELL ALL ADVERSE NAKED POSITIONS: $33,463 @ 3.0% = $1,004.00

CASH BALANCE WITH BROKERS – CREDIT $9,229

POSTSCRIPT

The previous analysis of the managed account was with respect to the position at the end of June 1973. Now all the options have expired that had been written at the end of June and it is possible to see precisely what transpired insofar as the positions at June 30 are concerned. Disregarding any new commitments, thereafter, this is what happened.

Item	Debit	Credit
Cost of securities purchased	$ 51,043	
Premiums from options sold		$ 28,231
Stocks purchased to cover naked calls/puts that were exercised.	50,303	
Sales proceeds of stocks bought to cover naked options		38,786
Sales proceeds of stocks long—options not exercised		18,816
Sales proceeds of stocks long—options exercised		6,039
Market value of stocks long—options expired and net of estimated brokerage cost to sell		9,072
	$101,346	$100,944
Loss		$402

Thus, as far as the windup of affairs with respect to the positions that existed at June 30, 1973, the combinations of losses on naked options and depreciation on the portfolio long in the account absorbed the premium income.

However, 1973 was a year of some despair as far as most equity investors were concerned. During the year well-known mutual funds, some of the most respected investment management names in the country, were down 25 percent to 50 percent. Hence the results were such that almost any equity portfolio manager in America would have been happy to achieve them.

14

Puts

A put is an option which gives its owner (the buyer) the right to require the seller (writer) of the put to purchase a particular stock at a fixed price during the option period. The put contract is a negotiable contract, bearing the endorsement of a member firm of the New York Stock Exchange. It is made out in bearer form and can be resold by one person to another. The following is a sample "put" option contract.

June 21, 1974

FOR VALUE RECEIVED, the BEARER may DELIVER to the endorser ONE HUNDRED (100) shares of the COMMON stock of the XYZ CORPORATION at Fifty dollars ($50.00) per share any TIME WITHIN 193 days from date.

THIS STOCK OPTION CONTRACT MUST BE PRESENTED, AS SPECIFIED BELOW, TO THE ENDORSING FIRM BEFORE THE EXPIRATION OF THE EXACT TIME LIMIT. IT CANNOT BE EXERCISED BY TELEPHONE.

DURING THE LIFE OF THIS OPTION:

1. (a)—The contract price hereof shall be reduced by the value of any cash dividend on the day the stock goes ex-dividend; (b)—where the Option is entitled to rights and/or warrants the contract price shall be reduced by the value of same as fixed by the opening sale thereof on the day the stock sells ex-rights or -warrants.

2. (a)—In the event of stock splits, reverse splits, or other similar action by the above-mentioned corporation, this Option shall become an Option for the equivalent in new securities when duly listed for trading and the total contract price shall not be reduced; (b)—stock dividends or the equivalent due-bills shall be attached to the stock covered hereby, when and if this option is exercised, and the total contract price shall not be reduced.

Upon presentation to the endorser of this option attached to a comparison ticket in the manner and time specified, the endorser agrees to accept notice of the Bearer's exercise by stamping the comparison, and this acknowledgment shall constitute a contract and shall be controlling with respect to delivery of the stock and settlement in accordance with New York Stock Exchange usage.

EXPIRES Dec. 31st 1974
3:15 P.M.

    Sold by member
    Put & Call
    Brokers & Dealers
    Association, Inc.

The undersigned acts as intermediary only without obligation other than to obtain a New York Stock Exchange firm as Endorser

Uses of Put Options to the Buyer

Why Buyers Buy Puts. A put can enable an investor to obtain a long-term capital gain on the bear side of the market (whereas a short sale cannot provide a long-term capital gain). A person in the higher tax brackets expects a particular stock to decline in value over the next six months or so. If he makes a short sale, and the stock declines in value, his profit would be a short-term gain, subject to full taxation. By purchase of a six-month-10-day put, he could realize the profit as tax-favored, long-term

110

capital gain. After holding the put for more than six months, he could sell it (back to his broker) and derive a long-term capital gain. If an anticipated drop in price does not develop, the put buyer has not traded in the particular stock and incurs no stock exchange commissions, as he would have in the case of a short sale.

Trading Against a Put. Using a put, a trader can seek to profit on price fluctuations in the stock by a number of trades with the knowledge that, at the time each trade takes place, he is fully protected against unlimited loss. A trader expects that XYZ selling at 100 will drop to 80 during the next six months, but thinks the decline will take place in a series of downward movements. He buys a put on XYZ at 100 for six months and ten days, paying $1,000. Thirty days later, XYZ drops to 88. The trader anticipating that the shares will rise temporarily before they fall again, buys 100 shares at 88. If XYZ continues to drop, he is protected by his put. He can deliver the 100 shares purchased at 88 for $100 per share by exercising his put. And so he cannot lose irrespective of how far the stock may decline during the option period. If his timing is correct, XYZ shares over the next 30 days will rise in value, let us say to 98; he then sells the shares bought at 88, and realizes a short-term profit of $1,000. Should XYZ drop again—e.g., to $87—he may repurchase in anticipation of profitable resale on another rise in price. Should such a rise above 87 not develop, he is fully protected by his put against loss resulting from decline below 87. If XYZ rallies and climbs above 87 the trader is able to secure another short-term profit. Each time he buys XYZ under the price of his put ($100) during the life of the option, he is guaranteed against loss from further decline while he seeks a trading profit from an increase in price. During the time the trader has been trading against the option, he also has an investment in the put. At expiry if the stock is selling over 100, the put premium is lost. However, he may have substantial profits on his purchases and sales against the put. If XYZ were selling below 100 but above 90, the put contract would have some value. So his loss would be less than the $1,000 cost of the put. If XYZ sold at 80 he would have a long-term capital gain of about 100 percent on his put in addition to the riskless profits made on trades during the option period against the put.

Buying Both a Convertible Bond and a Put. An investor buys a convertible bond and a put option. Each $1,000 convertible bond of XYZ is selling at 104 ($1,040). It is convertible into 20 shares of XYZ common. With XYZ common selling at 52, each bond at $1,040 sells at its conversion worth (20 shares times $52 per share). By buying five bonds, the trader establishes a position that is equivalent to holding 100 common shares (20 shares per bond times five bonds).

To buy five XYZ convertible bonds on 50 percent margin costs (in terms of cash outlay) $2,600 (i.e., 50 percent of $5,200). An investor buys 5 bonds on margin, paying $2,600. Simultaneously he purchases a six-month-ten-day put on XYZ common at 52, paying a $400 premium. The cost of a six-month-ten-day put is about 50 percent less than the cost of a call covering the same stock. He initially has out-of-pocket expenditures of $3,000 ($2,600 for bonds plus $400 for the put). Three possibilities then exist: (a) XYZ stock might remain at 52 when the put expires; (b) XYZ stock might appreciate in value; (c) XYZ might drop in value.

Situation (a). If XYZ is selling at 52 when the put is due to expire, the put will not be exercised and he will have a $400 long-term loss when the put expires. However, the bonds will probably not have lost any value. In this case, the investor has limited his loss to his expenses plus the $400-cost of the put (reduced by the value of any tax benefit).

Situation (b). Assume that XYZ stock climbs to 62. Again, the put lapses, causing a $400 loss. However, there is a substantial profit on the convertible bonds. When the position was taken in the five bonds, the bonds were selling for their conversion worth, 100 common shares at $52 each. With the common selling at 62, the unrealized appreciation should be at least $1,000 (10 point rise on 100 shares). The bonds should move up in value as the underlying common moved up to maintain conversion parity, and frequently will rise in value at a faster rate. The $1,000 reduced by $400 cost of the unexercised put gives a profit of $600 on an original investment of $3,000, about 40 percent return on an annual basis (exclusive of interest costs and interest income and brokerage expenses).

Situation (c). If XYZ stock drops in value, it is possible that the trader still might realize a substantial profit, and any possible loss is definitely limited. The investment in the bonds is $5,200, and with $400 cost for the put, the total investment is $5,600. By exercising the conversion privilege, he may obtain 100 shares during the option period and sell them for $5,200 through the put privilege. Thus, loss due to a decline in XYZ is limited to $400. However, if XYZ drops very substantially, he could probably realize a profit on the downside. Because of the investment value of the bonds without regard to conversion features, there would be a floor price under which they would not be expected to sell; i.e., the price at which comparable bonds without conversion privileges would be selling. Let us say that the "floor" for the bonds is $940. But if at the same time as the bonds decline to $940—total for five bonds, $4,700—XYZ stock drops from 52 to 32. The investor would: (a) sell the bonds for $4,700; buy 100 shares at 32; and (c) sell the 100 shares at 52. He would recover his put cost ($400) and the $500 drop in value in the bonds and still have a $1,100 gain through exercising the put because the profit through exercising the put is $2,000 (i.e., $52 less $32 per share times 100 shares).

The Put Option Used to Insure a Long Position. An investor attracted to XYZ stock, selling at 40, buys 100 shares and purchases a put for $500 exercisable at 40, which he identifies as insurance for his stock investment in his records.

If XYZ drops precipitously, from 40 to 10 over the next few months, he can deliver his shares to the seller of the put and recoup his $4,000. The put cost ($500) is added to the dollar cost of the shares sold ($4,000); total, $4,500. Thus, he has a $500 short-term capital loss when he exercises the put and receives the $4,000.

If XYZ appreciates in value, to 85, the put lapses unexercised. On the lapse of the put, the investor is not allowed any deduction. The cost of the put ($500) is added to the tax cost basis ($4,000) of the shares it insured. If the investor then sells the shares (more than six months after purchase) he will have a long-term capital gain of $4,000. The put insured the investor against a large capital loss while he sought tax-favored long-term capital gain. At the moment of making his investment, he established a limit on his potential capital loss through put insurance, although there was no ceiling on his possible long-term capital gain.

Year-End Tax Benefits from a Put. A put can be used to fix investment results in one year while deferring tax consequences to a future year, as the following two examples illustrate.

Example I. An investor is in a 50 percent tax bracket. He has already realized $10,000 short-term gains during the year and has realized no losses to offset such fully taxed gains. He thus is in a position to incur taxes of $5,000. To offset such gains, he takes $10,000 of long-term losses by selling from his portfolio. By offsetting long-term losses against his short-term gains he avoids a $5,000 tax. He also holds in his portfolio a stock, AGE, on which he has a $10,000 long-term gain. Because of market conditions, he thinks it advisable to sell. But if he realizes such long-term gains this year, his long-term losses would have to be offset against this tax-favored long-term gain, leaving his short-term profits of $10,000 subject to tax at

50 percent. Taking his long-term profits on AGE this year requires him to use $10,000 long-term losses to avoid about $2,500 long-term tax instead of $5,000 short-term taxes. There is a method by which he can use his long-term losses against his short-term gains this year and still protect his gain (long-term profits) in AGE but postpone the tax thereon until next year.

He purchases a put, covering his AGE shares with an option period that extends into next year. The put freezes his long-term profit at current market price, but he does not realize such profit for tax purposes until he exercises his put next year. This year his long-term losses offset his short-term gains, but without market risk, and the AGE sale is postponed. He could also postpone recognition of the long-term gain in AGE without risk due to a decline in price by selling short against the box and in the new year using the long position to cover the short. However, if AGE declines, as expected, and the put were sold more than six months after purchase, the gain from the put (after costs) would be long term. The short sale against the box, when covered, produces a short-term gain.

Example II. An investor has held for less than six months 100 shares of stock which cost $9,000 but which are now worth $15,000. His profit is short-term. He believes it advisable to take that profit this year. However, he has had a profitable year and his $6,000 short-term profit will be taxed at very high rates when added to his other income. Next year he expects the same $6,000 short-term profit to be subject to a lower tax when added to his other income. Although a put cannot be used to convert his short-term profit into a long-term one, it can be used to freeze his investment profit at current market price and at the same time defer tax until next year. He buys a put with an option duration which extends into next year. In the next year he exercises his put. He has frozen the amount of his profit—which is still short-term. However, he has shifted that profit from a high-income year to a lower-income year and therefore it is subject to reduced tax rates.

Buying a Put to Protect a Profit from the Purchase of a Call. When XYZ is selling at 40, an investor buys a six-month-ten-day call for $800. After 3 months, XYZ sells at 60. Before expenses and taxes he can sell his call for a $1,200 profit, but the profit would be a short-term capital gain. In seeking greater profit from further appreciation of XYZ and also to allow the profit to become long-term gain, he buys a 90-day put on XYZ at 60 for a cost of $300. He is now assured of $900 before expenses because, during the option period, he can exercise his call, obtain 100 shares of XYZ at 40, which he could then sell for 60 by exercising his put. If XYZ fell to 40, the call would be worthless, and lapses, causing a $800 loss. However, the $300 put now has a value of $2,000. He can sell the put, recoup his $1,100 cost for both options, and net $900 (before expenses and taxes). The $900 is a short-term capital gain.

If XYZ continued to climb (after the purchase of the call at 40 and a put at 60) and at the end of six months sells at 70, the call would have a value of $3,000, which upon sale probably produces a long-term capital gain. (Check with your tax advisor to verify the current status). The put would be worthless.

At the end of six months after the purchase of the put, XYZ stock has dropped in value from the put striking price of 60 but still sells above 40, the price at which the call is exercisable. Revenue is produced from both options, totaling $2,000 less expenses and the $1,100 cost of the options.

Adjustments to Put Option Exercise Price. *Rights.* When rights are issued on a stock covered by a put option, the put option price is reduced by an amount equal to the price at which the first sale of the rights is made on the day that the particular stock sells ex-rights.

Dividends. The put option exercise price is reduced by the amount of cash dividends. This adjustment to the option price is made on the day that the stock goes "ex" a cash dividend.

Stock Dividends and Splits. Adjustments are also required in the case of stock dividends and stock splits. In the case of a stock split the number of shares covered by the option is doubled. The same type of adjustment is made in the case of a stock dividend. If a 10 percent stock dividend is declared during the option period the owner of a put would have to deliver 110 shares of stock to exercise the put. In the case of cash dividends and stock rights, downward adjustment is made in the striking price. In the case of stock dividends and stock splits, the number of shares covered by the option is increased.

Writers of Put Options

Selling Put Options. The seller of a put receives a premium from the buyer for which the seller is obligated to purchase 100 shares of stock at the agreed price for the time period specified.

The position of a "naked" put seller is comparable in some ways to that of a seller of a call who is long in the stock. In both cases the potential profit from the premium received is realized profit provided the stock remains at the striking price or increases. In other words, it is a "bull" market technique when a "naked" put is sold.

Example. Sale of a naked put. Sell one put for six months ten days on XYZ at 50 for a premium of $500. The seller of the put assumes that the price of XYZ will not drop below 50 and that the option will expire unexercised. In such event, the put-writer's return on investment (ROI) is calculated as follows:

Minimum margin requirement at 25% of $5,000 market value of underlying XYZ stock	$1,250
Less: premium received	(500)
Cash outlay	$ 750

$$\text{ROI} = \frac{\$500 \text{ (premium)}}{\$750 \text{ (cash outlay)}} \times \frac{365 \text{ (days)}}{193 \text{ (days)}} = \underline{\underline{126\%}}$$

The margin requirement exists even though the writer's brokerage account has no debit balance (i.e., no borrowed funds are involved). Such requirement may be met by the deposit of cash or of other marginable securities such that the combined loan value of securities and cash equals $1,250. In the event that the price of XYZ rises, the option writer's margin requirement increases adversely as the requirement will continue to be at least 25 percent of the then higher market value of XYZ and, in addition, through the "mark-to-market" process, each $100 of price increase over $5,000 of XYZ adds $100 to the margin requirement. (If XYZ falls below 50, margin requirements are similarly reduced.)

In the event that XYZ falls and the put option is exercised, the writer's gain is reduced or his loss increased by the two brokerage commissions he must pay—(a) to buy when the XYZ shares are put to him and (b) to sell the XYZ shares so acquired. A $3.00 decrease in XYZ shares below 50 would have the following effect:

Premium	$500
Less: 2 brokerage commissions	(130)*
Less: adverse price movement (100 shares at $3.00 per share)	(300)
Gain	$ 70

*Excludes SEC fee and N.Y. transfer tax.

The ROI with such $3 drop in XYZ is:

$$\frac{\$70 \text{ gain}}{\$750 \text{ outlay}} \times \frac{365 \text{ days}}{193 \text{ days}} = \underline{\underline{17.6\%}}$$

Sale of a Hedged Put. The put option may also be sold in conjunction with a short sale of the same security on which the put is sold. For example, sell one put for six months ten days on XYZ at 50 for a premium of $500 and simultaneously sell short 100 XYZ at 50. In this case, if the stock declines, the gain on the short sale is balanced by the loss on the sale of the put, and the investor profits by the premium (less expenses). The ROI provided the stock remains at 50 or has declined at the option expiry is calculated as follows:

Margin requirements: 65% of $5,000*	$3,250
Less: premium received	500
Cash outlay	$2,750

*(No margin requirement exists for the put in this instance as it is hedged by the short sale—as in the case of a call sold against a long position.)

$$\text{ROI} = \frac{\$500 \text{ less } \$130 \text{ brokerage}^1}{\$2,750 \text{ cash outlay}} \times \frac{365 \text{ days}}{193 \text{ days}} = \underline{25\%}$$

The put striking price in this case would be further reduced by dividends, if any, on XYZ stock and the person in the short sale position must pay (to the lender) the cash dividends declared—even though not received—on the stock borrowed to effect the short sale.

Taxes on Put Options

Sale of a Put. When a put is sold, the premium paid to the writer is not income upon receipt. The tax consequences are delayed. If the put expires without being exercised, the premium then becomes ordinary income to the writer. If the put is exercised, the premium previously received by the writer reduces the cost of the stock he is required to buy. The writer of the exercised put is considered to have purchased stock at a reduced cost price but does not realize current income due to the premium.

---

[1] Excludes SEC fee and N.Y. transfer tax.

Purchase of a Put. There are no tax consequences from the purchase of a put until the transaction is closed. (a) If the buyer of a put later sells it he has a capital gain or loss. That gain or loss is long-term or short-term depending upon whether he has held the put for more than six months. (b) If the buyer of the put lets it lapse unexercised, he has a capital loss in the amount he paid for the put. That loss will be long-term or short-term depending upon whether the put has been held for more than six months when it expires unexercised. However, an exception arises when the put buyer also purchases 100 shares of the related stock on the same day—which he intends to use for delivery—if he should later exercise the put. Then, the cost of the put is added to the tax cost of the 100 related shares of stock, if the put is allowed to lapse unexercised. Under the exception, if the put is exercised, the put buyer sells 100 shares of the related stock at the option price, fixed by the put. In such case, he subtracts the amount paid for the put from the proceeds realized on the sale of the stock. On the exercise of a put, a long-term or short-term transaction results depending upon how long the stock used in delivery was held.

In one circumstance, a put sale is treated specially to prevent one from changing a short-term profit to a long-term profit without economic risk. This provision is aimed at preventing an investor from converting a fully taxed short-term profit to a tax-favored long-term gain. For example, an investor has held 100 shares of XYZ stock for five months and has a substantial profit. To freeze the profit and allow it to become a long-term gain in due course, he buys a put covering such shares, allowing him to sell at the current market price during the option period. He exercises the put two months after purchase and delivers the XYZ shares. Although he has held the XYZ shares for seven months, his profit in this situation is treated as a short-term gain. In addition, if he lets the put lapse without exercising it in this situation and sells

XYZ shares in the open market at a profit, his profit could still be a short-term gain. A put cannot be used to convert a short-term gain into a long-term one, nor can a put be used to convert a long-term loss into a short-term loss.

Summary

The purchase of a put offers many possible advantages either as an insurance hedge to protect one's position or as an investment speculation. For a reasonable cost, the premium, the put buyer derives considerable potential benefit. On the other hand, for a premium the writer of a naked put assumes considerable risk. A writer of hedged options must weigh the profit potential of (1) selling calls against long positions (risk on downside) as compared with (2) selling puts against short positions (risk on upside). If an option writer wishes the risk to be on the upside (bear writer), he must weigh the profit potential and risk of selling a naked call against the possibilities through the sale of a hedged put.

Both sides of an actual put option contract are shown in the accompanying illustrations.

FIGURE 14-1

1105

NEGOTIATED BY
Ragnar Option Corporation
PUT AND CALL OPTIONS
GUARANTEED BY MEMBERS N Y STOCK EXCHANGE
39 BROADWAY, N.Y. 10006 (212) 248-2460

New York, N.Y. SEPT. 28 1973

For Value Received, the BEARER may DELIVER to the endorser ONE HUNDRED (100) shares of the COMMON stock of the ATLANTIC RICHFIELD CO - THE - at NINETY FIVE AND THREE EIGHTS Dollars ($ 95.375) per share ANY TIME WITHIN **96** days from date.

The Endorser agrees to accept notice of Bearer's exercise by stamping the comparison ticket attached to this Option ONLY when it is presented to the cashier of the endorsing firm in the manner and within the time specified.

This acknowledgment shall constitute a contract and shall be controlling with respect to delivery and settlement in accordance with Stock Exchange usage and the agreement on the reverse side hereof.

THIS OPTION CANNOT BE EXERCISED BY TELEPHONE
EXPIRES JAN.07 74 (date) 3:15 P.M. (time)

New York, N.Y. Time
(Standard Option Contract)

The undersigned acts as intermediary only, without obligation other than to obtain a New York Stock Exchange firm as Endorser.

SEAL

Ragnar Option Corporation

No. R10759

PUT OPTION

COPYRIGHT 1973

FIGURE 14-2

AGREEMENT

1. (a) On the day the stock goes ex-dividend, the contract price hereof shall be reduced by the value of any cash dividend.
(b) On the day that the stock sells ex-rights and/or warrants, the contract price hereof shall be reduced by the value of the same as fixed by the opening sale thereof, provided that the option is entitled to said rights and/or warrants

2. (a) The total contract price shall not be reduced in the event of stock splits, reverse splits, or exchanges of securities, or other similar action by the above mentioned corporation, and this option shall become an option for the equivalent in new securities when duly listed for trading.
(b) When and if this option is exercised stock dividends, or the equivalent due bills shall be attached to the stock covered and the total price of this contract shall not be reduced thereby.

PRESCOTT, BALL & TURBEN
ONE BATTERY PARK PLAZA
NEW YORK, N. Y. 10004

Endorsed by:

PRESCOTT, BALL & TURBEN
BY
PARTNER

Members of the New York Stock Exchange

15

Straddles, Spreads, Strips, Straps, Special Options, and Conversions

Straddles

A straddle is both a put and a call at the same striking price, usually the market price of the stock at the time the option is written.

If neither side of the combined option is exercised, that is neither the put nor the call side, the issuer or seller of the straddle obtains a short-term capital gain for the entire premium he received for selling the combined option. This income is realized when the unexercised straddle lapses.

The buyer of the straddle has a capital loss reflecting the entire price he paid for the combined option—if he does not exercise either the put or the call. The capital loss is suffered when the unexercised straddle lapses. It is a long-term or short-term loss depending upon whether the straddle had been held for more than six months when it expired.

Any time during the option duration, the holder can

exercise either the put or call, if it is to his benefit. He may even exercise both. When one or both sides of the straddle are exercised the writer should allocate the premium he received between the put and call, based on their respective market values at the time the straddle was issued. After such allocation, the put and the call are treated as separate options. If one side and only one side—either the put or the call—is unexercised, the portion of the premium allocated to that unexercised side of the option is a short-term gain.

Examples. A writer sells a straddle for $500 and allocates the premium as follows: to the call, $275 and to the put, $225.

Example I. Assume that, during the option period, the call is exercised and the put expires. The writer sells 100 shares to the holder of the call. The writer adds $275 to the amount he receives on sale of the stock to increase his capital gain or decrease any capital loss on the sale. The writer reports $225 as a short-term gain on the lapse of the put.

The buyer of the option adds $275, the value attributed to the call, to his tax cost on purchase of the stock acquired when the call is exercised. The value allocated to the put, $225, which lapses, is a capital loss, long-term or short-term, depending on whether the option was held for more than six months at the time of lapse.

Example II. If, during the option period, only the put is exercised, the writer buys 100 shares offered by the holder of the option. The writer reduces his cost basis of the stock purchased by the value attributed to the put, $225, and ultimately increases any gain or decreases any loss on the subsequent sale of the stock. The writer reports $275 as short-term gain on the lapse of the unexpired call side of the option. The buyer of the option subtracts from the proceeds realized on the sale of stock a $225 amount to decrease tax on any gain realized from the profitable exercise of the put. The value originally allocated to the call, $275, produces a capital loss when the buyer's unexercised call lapses, which loss is long-term or short-term depending on whether the option was held for more than six months.

Example III. If the stock fluctuates sharply and both the call and the put are exercised, the writer adds $275 to the amount he receives from sale of the stock on exercise of the call, increasing his gain or decreasing his loss on the sale. The writer also reduces the tax cost of the stock purchased by him on exercise of the put by $225. Such reduction in tax basis on the purchased shares will eventually increase his taxable gain or decrease his loss on the sale of those shares. The buyer of the option, on exercising the call, adds $275 to his cost basis of the stock he purchases, which ultimately decreases any taxable gain or increases any deductible loss on the eventual sale of the stock. He deducts $225 from the amount received on sale of the stock acquired when the put is exercised, decreasing any taxable gain and increasing any loss from such sale.

If either or both sides of the straddle are exercised the price received for the straddle is required to be allocated to the put portion and the call portion, based on the market values at the time the straddle was written. Because it may be difficult to determine such values the Internal Revenue Service will allow a 55-percent–45-percent apportionment of the premium. The writer and buyer may allocate 55 percent to the call and 45 percent to the put. If a straddle is sold for $1,000, the seller could allocate $550 to the call and $450 to the put. The seller is not required to use this formula. He can allocate the premium based on market value.

Writing a Straddle. Seven months ago an investor bought XYZ shares at 95, which currently sell at 100. On sale of such shares now, he could obtain a long-term profit of $5 per share. Assume he is willing to sell his shares at a price higher than current market, and that he also would not object to adding another 100 shares to his portfolio if he can buy such shares at below the current market price. By the sale of a straddle, exercisable at 100, the benefits of one of these two possibilities might be obtained. Or if the benefits of neither are realized he could obtain extra income from his holding of XYZ shares.

Assume that he sells a 90-day straddle on the shares for $1,000. In the event that the buyer of the straddle exercises it in whole, or in part, he is willing to allocate $550 of the $1,000 received for the straddle to the call and $450 to the put. One of four things will occur; the call is exercised, the put is exercised, neither is exercised, or both are exercised.

1. The call is exercised because XYZ rises. He sells stock costing $9,500 for the sum of $10,550 ($10,000 plus $550 of the premium). He has thus sold his shares at a long-term capital gain of $1,050. In addition, he has a short-term gain of $450 from the lapsed put.

2. The put is exercised because XYZ decreases. He will be required to pay $10,000 for 100 shares at a time when the market price is less—e.g., $9,500. Of the $1,000 premium that he received for selling the straddle, he allocates $450 to the put which is exercised. That reduces the cost of the put shares to $9,550. However, he has a $550 short-term gain on the call which lapsed.

3. Neither side of the straddle is exercised. At the end of the option period the stock still sells at 100. The writer received $1,000 in premium, all of which is ordinary income.

4. Both sides of the straddle are exercised. In this case the premiums allocated to the put and to the call are treated in the ordinary manner for a single put or a single call—i.e., as an adjustment to the cost basis. For the call, the premium is added to the sales proceeds when the stock is called away. For the put, the premium is deducted from the price paid to acquire the stock being put to the writer.

Spreads

A spread is similar to a straddle in that it consists of a call and a put. However there are different striking prices for the two options. Thus, a straddle at 50 would give the buyer a put and a call at 50. A 2-point spread, however, gives the buyer a put at 49 and a call at 51. The premium received by the seller of a spread is normally reduced (compared to premium from a straddle) by about $50 for each point of spread. So, if the seller of a straddle at 50 would receive a premium of $600, the seller of a 2-point spread, exercisable at 49 and 51, would probably receive about $500. The spread option is not commonly traded. A spread increases the possibilities that neither side of the option will be exercised, and, if neither is exercised, the seller reports the premium as ordinary income.

The Strip and the Strap

A strip is a straddle with an extra put; i.e., two puts and one call. A strip at $100 would require the seller to buy 200 shares at 100 or sell 100 shares at the same price. A strip is more expensive, of course, than a straddle.

A strap is one put and two calls; i.e., it is a straddle with an extra call. Normally, a strap will be more expensive than the strip. The premiums for both strips and straps also are allocated among the components on the basis of the respective values.

The profit on the lapse of one of the parts of a strip or strap results in a short-term gain, if an identification test is met. The premium on the sale of a strap is allocated to each of the calls and the put on the basis of the respective values, after which one call and the put are identified as constituting a straddle. If the buyer exercises the two calls and allows the put to lapse the profit on the expired put is short-term gain. However, if the put is exercised and the calls both lapse, the amount of premium allocated to the call previously identified as part of the straddle is a short-term gain. But the premium from the call that is not part of the straddle is ordinary income.

Special Option Offers

Special options are option contracts which were bought originally by an option dealer in the expectation that he could resell the contracts at a profit. Such special options are offered by put and call brokers. In addition to arranging the sale and purchase of new options, such brokers often carry an inventory of existing options which they offer for sale. Special options are offered normally at a striking price different from the current market price of the stock. The striking price of newly issued options usually is fixed at the market price at the time the option is negotiated. However, for special options, it is probable that the market price of the particular stock underlying the option will differ from the striking price of the special option, because of the lag between the time of the original issuance of the special option contract and the time at which the contract is being reoffered. Also, in addition to the price difference, the duration of the option will differ from the normal 35-, 65- and 95-day periods. Since a special option has already been in existence for some time, the remaining period at the time of the special offering will not correspond to the usual time periods for newly issued options.

Special options will be priced according to their terms, and will vary from the prices for newly issued options according to their terms. For example, a special call at 100 will sell at a price in excess of $1,000 if the underlying stock has risen to 110. Unlike a new call, the special call already reflects a gain of 10 points. However, since part of the option term has expired, that fact will tend to reduce the price of the special.

Shown in figure 15-1 are offerings of an option dealer of both special puts and special calls.

FIGURE 15-1

PUT

SPECIAL OPTIONS

subject to prior sale or price change

22⅞	AMF INC	19⅞	AUG	14	$162.50
8⅝	AMER BLD M	9½	AUG	12	150.00
15⅝	AUSTRAL OIL	17⅝	APR	4	375.00
82	ASA LTD	91½	APR	1	1275.00
36⅝	BAUSCH & L	35⅞	MAY	20	275.00
23½	BELL & HOW	22	JUN	7	250.00
17¾	BOWMAR ..	18⅞	JUN	4	400.00
93¾	COMB ENGR	96¾	JUN	13	1500.00
29⅞	COPPER RNG	30	JUN	3	400.00
46¼	DEERE	48	JUN	17	687.50
24¼	FLYING TIGR	22	JUN	10	200.00
14⅞	EG & G	14	JUN	3	150.00
106¾	JOHN & JOHN	107⅞	APR	29	887.50
74⅞	HONEYWELL	75½	JUN	17	987.50
83⅞	H'STAKE MIN	86½	APR	15	775.00
47⅝	NATOMAS ...	48⅞	MAY	8	687.50
105⅜	PHIL MORRIS	111	APR	15	1050.00
41¾	MGIC INV ...	38¾	APR	25	287.50
18¼	T W A	15¾	SEP	3	187.50
17⅛	WANG LAB ..	17⅝	SEP	16	325.00
43	US STEEL ..	38⅝	JUL	29	137.50

CALLS

22⅞	AMF	19⅞	AUG	14	$525.00
10¾	ADD MULTI .	10¼	AUG	2	287.50
82	ASA LTD	93¼	AUR	8	287.50
23½	BELL & HOW	22	JUN	7	350.00
17¾	BOWMAR ...	18⅞	JUN	4	275.00
17⅜	COX BDCSTG	17¼	JUN	10	250.00
14⅛	CURTISS WRT	11⅛	APR	9	375.00
93¾	COMB ENGR	96¾	JUN	13	675.00
29⅞	COPPER RNG	30	JUN	3	387.50
46¼	DEERE ...	48	JUN	7	487.50
14¼	FLEXI VAN .	11½	AUG	26	387.50
14	GLOBAL MAR	15⅛	MAY	7	137.50
106¾	JOHN & JOHN	107⅞	APR	29	750.00
47⅝	NATOMAS ..	48⅞	MAY	8	587.50
43⅛	LA LAND & E	44½	AUG	5	350.00
7¼	MCCULL OIL	7¼	JUL	18	150.00
105⅜	PHIL MORRIS	111	APR	15	487.50
14⅞	NORT SIMON	14⅛	AUG	21	325.00
8¼	RITE AID	8	SEP	6	225.00
20⅞	SPRAGUE ...	18⅝	APR	29	387.50
18¼	T W A	18	6 MOS.		350.00
43	US STEEL ...	38⅛	JUL	19	625.00

RagnaR

OPTION CORPORATION

26 Broadway

N.Y..N.Y.10004•(212) 248-2460

MEMBER CHICAGO BOARD OPTIONS EXCHANGE

OUT OF AREA CALL TOLL FREE (800) 221-2267

CALL

SPECIAL OPTIONS

subject to prior sale or price change plus tax.

21⅛	AMF INC ..	20	AUG.	14	$425.00
10⅛	ADD MULTIGRAPH	10¼	AUG.	2	162.50
12⅝	APACHE	15½	JULY	17	100.00
87⅞	ASA LTD	96	AUG.	26	1100.00
34½	BAUSCH & LOMB .	38⅜	JUNE	10	275.00
21¼	BELL & HOWELL ..	22	JUNE	7	225.00
13	CLOROX ..	13	AUG.	12	275.00
17⅜	COX BROADCAST ..	17¼	JUNE	10	200.00
29⅜	COPPER RANGE	29¼	JUNE	3	375.00
49¾	DISNEY	53⅝	APR.	18	275.00
42¾	DEERE	48	JUNE	17	225.00
33⅜	FREE STATES ..	34⅜	MAY	14	375.00
15⅛	GEN INSTRUMENT	15¼	MAY	31	250.00
15¾	HOLIDAY INNS	14⅞	AUG.	12	275.00
49¾	NATOMAS	48⅞	MAY	8	625.00
102	PHILIP MORRIS	103¾	MAY	6	675.00
16⅝	NORTON SIMON	14⅛	AUG.	21	387.50
20	RCA CORP ...	19⅛	AUG.	1	287.50
15⅝	TRANS WORLD AIR	18	SEPT.	18	225.00
16¾	WANG LAB	17⅝	SEPT.	16	325.00

PUTS

21⅛	AMF INC	21½	JUNE	10	$275.00
12⅝	APACHE	15½	JUNE	17	350.00
87⅞	ASA LTD ...	83¼	APR.	15	275.00
34½	BAUSCH & LOMB .	40⅜	MAY	2	725.00
21¼	BELL & HOWELL	23½	JUNE	14	350.00
16	BOWMAR ..	18⅞	JUNE	4	387.50
84¼	COMBUSTION ENG	97	JUNE	13	1800.00
29⅜	COPPER RANGE ..	30	JUNE	3	375.00
49¾	DISNEY	53⅝	APR.	18	575.00
42¾	DEERE	48	JUNE	17	775.00
20¼	FLYING TIGER	27	JUNE	10	325.00
33⅜	FREE STATES	34⅝	MAY	17	387.50
22⅞	GULF OIL	22¼	AUG.	2	212.50
13¾	EG&G	17¼	AUG.	12	487.50
13¾	EG&G	12⅝	AUG.	30	162.50
111¼	JOHNSON&JOHNSON	107⅞	APR.	29	525.00
40½	LA LAND & EXPL	47	MAY	16	825.00
6½	MCCULLOCH OIL	7¼	JULY	18	225.00
102	PHILIP MORRIS	111	APR.	15	1150.00
18¼	SPRAGUE ELECT	19¾	APR.	8	375.00
15⅝	TRANS WORLD AIR	15¾	SEPT.	3	287.50
42⅛	UV IND	39⅞	APR.	17	112.50
14⅝	WESTERN UNION	15¼	JULY	15	475.00

RagnaR

OPTION CORPORATION

26 Broadway

N.Y..N.Y.10004•(212) 248-2460

MEMBER CHICAGO BOARD OPTIONS EXCHANGE

OUT OF AREA CALL TOLL FREE (800) 221-2267

Option Conversions

Investors generally tend to be bullish. This, then, means that there is generally a greater demand for call options than for puts. And call options on a stock, all things being equal, are normally more expensive than put options. It is sometimes the case that a put and call dealer, in order to satisfy the demand from buyers of call options, may do so by locating writers of puts or straddles on the particular stock. This may be accomplished through a process termed *conversion*. Conversion is the process by which a put may be transformed into a call or vice versa.

Converting a Put to a Call. An investor wishes to buy a six-month-ten-day call on XYZ at 50 and is willing to pay a premium of $650. His put and call broker is unable to find a seller of such a call but does find a writer willing to sell a put for a premium of $340. A stock exchange member firm agrees to act as the converter, and it purchases the put for $365 from the put and call dealer. It simultaneously buys the stock for $5,000. The member firm then sells a call, as desired, for a premium of $600 from the put and call dealer. The writer of the put has received a premium of $340 from the put and call dealer, who retains $25 as a markup. The buyer of the call has received at a cost of $675 that which he desired. The put and call dealer retains a $50 markup on the sale of the call ($650 received from the buyer less $600 paid to the member firm).

The position, then, of the put seller is that he has received the premium he desired from the sale of the put. The position of the call buyer is that he has the sought-after call at the agreed premium. The position of the put and call dealer is that it has simply acted as dealer and derived gross income of $25 from the sale of the put and $50 from the sale of the call.

The more complicated position is that of the member firm, the converter. It has a riskless position and is assured of a gross profit of $235. It will realize $235 no matter what happens to the price of the XYZ stock. The member firm's situation is as follows. It owns a put acquired for $365 that allows it to sell, during the next six months and ten days, 100 shares XYZ at 50; i.e., $5,000 for 100 shares. It has purchased 100 shares of XYZ at 50 for a total cost of $5,000, presumably paying no commission to purchase the shares. (Technically the converter would have nominal expenses to the Exchange, transfer tax, SEC fee, and certain other small expenses which are disregarded.) It has sold for $600 a six-month-ten-day call on XYZ, exercisable at 50. If XYZ increases above 50 and the call is exercised, the member firm receives back its $5,000 and delivers the 100 shares. It is ahead the difference between the $600 from the call less the $365 paid for its put, a total of $235.

Assuming that the call is exercised at or near the end of the option period—i.e., one-half year—then the rate of return on investment to the member firm is: $235 gain times 2 (to obtain annual return) divided by the $5,000 investment tied up in owning 100 shares, or 9.4 percent annually. However, in the event that the call is exercised at an early date, and the converter has $5,000 tied up for proportionately less time, its rate of return is that much higher. In addition, in the event that the call is exercised early, the broker still retains its put and has the potential profit that may arise from its possession throughout the duration of the option period.

If XYZ falls in value, the call will simply expire unexercised, as the call buyer obviously will not exercise it if XYZ is at 50 or below. In this case the member firm exercises its put option to sell 100 shares for $5,000, thus recovering its invested capital and disposing of the shares. Here, too, the member firm's profit is $235, the difference between the receipt from the sale of the call and the payment to acquire the put.

In the rare event that XYZ remains at 50, or fractionally higher at the moment when the call expires unexercised, the shares could simply be sold on the market.

Investors or traders may follow a similar process to convert their own options and the ability to do so can mean increased profits or protection. For example, an investor buys a 95-day call on X stock at 40, paying a premium of $300. After the elapse of 35 days X is at 50. The investor thinks the stock will fall. To capture his gain on the call and in order to benefit from a decline in X below 50, he requests a put and call broker to convert his call into a put.

Since the call still has 60 days before expiration and has a value of $1,000 ($10 per share on 100 shares), a converter (member firm) is willing to buy it. At the same time, the member firm sells 100 X short at the current price of 50. It also delivers to the dealer a put on X at 40 that expires in 60 days. (The put is at the same striking price and same expiry date as the original call.) Together with the put, the member firm delivers $900 to the put and call dealer. The dealer then delivers to the customer the put option and $875, thus deducting $25 for handling the transaction.

The position of the various parties is then as follows.

The investor's position: Cash expended $300; cash received $875. He owns one put, 60 days, on X at 40.

The put and call broker's position: He received $900 from the converter, paid $875 to the investor, and he has no risk.

The situation of the converter: He owns a call at 40 for 60 days (stock is at 50), is short 100 X at 50, and expended $900 (to the put and call broker); and he sold one put, expiring in 60 days, at 40.

The investor has a cash flow of $575 plus any additional amount he will receive from exercising the put if X falls below $40. The put and call broker's cash flow is $25. The converter's position is the most complex. However, the converter makes at least $100 before expenses no matter what X stock may do. At prices of X of above 40, he exercises his call at 40 and the shares received are delivered to close out the short sale at 50, producing $1,000. This sum less $900 expended provides $100 (for tying up no money—only the margin requirement in terms of a collateral deposit on the short sale must be met). The put sold at 40 lapses.

At prices of X below 40, the converter lets his call lapse, buys 100 shares put to him at 40, and uses those shares to close out the previous short sale at 50, a gain of $1,000 from which the $900 previously expended is deducted.

16

Conclusion

As recently as 1973, few investors understood the options market, and fewer still had ever invested. But since the spring of 1973 when the Chicago Board Options Exchange commenced, options have suddenly gained popularity. The CBOE trades only in calls, not puts, and at January 1974 traded only in calls of 32 stocks. Nevertheless, volume amounted to more than 800,000 contracts in its first six and one-half months in business.

Two institutions, seeking to provide a play in options to modest investors, have filed registration statements with the Security and Exchange Commission for closed-end option funds.

Probably in the near future the number of companies on which calls may be bought on the CBOE will expand greatly, and puts will probably be traded as well. Moreover, growth is changing the nature of the participants in the options market. Traditionally, the writers of options have been wealthy individuals and the buyers reasonably sophisticated investors. Now more institutions are being drawn into the market, attracted by the attractive return that writers hope to make. As more investors become option writers, the premiums on an option may fall, making the market still more attractive to buyers.

The Security and Exchange Commission will be examining the options markets to determine whether other exchanges should be allowed to trade options and whether option trading is adequately regulated, whether capital is being diverted from the stock market, and whether the liquidity of the underlying stocks is being affected.

Nothing remains static for long in the securities business, and options are no exception. Everything changes: margin requirements, interest rates, brokerage house rules, tax laws, patterns of premiums for options, and so on. Consequently, consider this book a guide which needs to be updated by the reader, constantly, to reflect the ever-changing pattern of all the variables involved.

The tremendous utility of options—for both buyers and writers—makes knowledge of them a tool with which every investor should be familiar, and chances are that options are a tool that will continue to command increasing interest.

Appendix 1

Regulatory and Legal Matters

REGULATORY AND LEGAL MATTERS

An option constitutes a security separate and apart from the security to which the option relates. A security (option) under certain circumstances must be registered with the SEC and with State regulatory bodies. However, the SEC expert on options indicates that the SEC is not taking any action against the writer's or registered brokers of options for failure to register such options as securities.

Nevertheless, the buyer of an option could bring a legal action against the writer in connection with Federal or State statutes requiring registration, and several such actions are in the courts, but no decisions have been rendered.

Options written on the CBOE are registered with the SEC and presumably in all states. Therefore, the buyer of a CBOE option could not be expected to have a claim against a writer in connection with failure to register such options pursuant to the provisions of Federal and State securities laws.

Various exemptions exist in Federal and State law allowing the sale of an unregistered security and it is quite possible that a writer of options (not on exchanges such as the CBOE) would have a valid defense against any suit by a buyer resulting from such statutory exemptions.

An option buyer might also bring suit against the broker who sold him an unregistered security,.i.e., an option not registered on an exchange. In this case, assuming an exemption were available to the writer of the option, such exemption might not be available to the broker (due to the relatively large number of transactions of the broker compared to those of a single writer).

Readers are cautioned to rely solely upon their own legal counsel for advice with respect to these matters. The foregoing discussion is included merely to acquaint the reader with the general situation.

Two rules, 9(b)(2) and 238, have been proposed to the Federal '34 Act and Securities Act by the SEC to clarify certain of these matters, but such rules have not yet been declared effective.

Index

Strap, 123, 127
Strategy, 67
Striking price, 1, 9
Strip, 123, 127
Supply, 71

T-V

Tax, 15, 25, 49, 86, 114, 119
Tax loss, 28
Technical analysis, 8
Transfer tax, 2

Utilities, 29
Vetco, 19
Volatility, 71

W-Y

Wall Street Journal, The, 77
Whipsaw, 70
Winnebago, 19
Writer, 15, 27, 117, 125
Year-end tax benefit, 114
Yield, 22